Ibiza and Minorca

by the same author
—

THE IONIAN ISLANDS
MAJORCA

Ibiza and Minorca

ARTHUR FOSS

FABER AND FABER LIMITED
3 Queen Square London

First published in 1975
by Faber and Faber Limited
3 Queen Square London WC1
Printed in Great Britain by
W & J Mackay Limited, Chatham
All rights reserved

ISBN 0 571 10487 8

For Bill and Margaret

Contents

Contents

Maps

Illustrations

The author wishes to thank Hugh Gibb for permission to reproduce photographs 4b, 7b and 8b, he himself being responsible for the rest. He also wishes to thank Norman Head for invaluable help in preparing these photographs for publication.

Preface

The original intention was that a book should be written about the Balearic Islands as a whole which, with their culture and scenery set against the blue sea and sky of the Mediterranean, form one of the most dazzling jewels in the crown of Spain. A brief examination, however, of the culture and historical background of these three islands—Majorca, Minorca and Ibiza—quickly suggested that justice could not be done to the group in one volume. Because of its size, its scenic grandeur and because of, among other reasons, its architectural and artistic treasures, it was decided to devote a single book to Majorca; it appeared with the title *Majorca* in 1972.

Ibiza and Minorca is my second and alas, concluding book about the Balearics. These islands are as intriguing and have an historical past as fascinating as Majorca. In Ibiza, as befits Carthage's first established colony, there is an abundance of relics of the Punic civilization. Its scenery in parts equals and on occasion even surpasses that of the wonderful north-west coastline of Majorca. Its whitewashed fortress churches are unique in Spain. Minorca possesses an immense treasury of prehistoric stone monuments in various stages of preservation. Although less mountainous than the other islands, there are stretches of coastline of very great beauty. Minorca was a British possession for much of the eighteenth century, a few signs of which still remain.

This book is meant to be self-contained. On occasion, however, one island will be found to have been far more richly endowed in a particular field than another. Majorca, for example, has virtually a monopoly of the works of its own mediaeval school of painting. There are two examples of this school in Ibiza cathedral which are discussed in the Ibicencan section of this book; no attempt however is here made to describe the Majorcan mediaeval school, as a chapter on this subject was included in the earlier book on Majorca. There are brief accounts in *Majorca* of the island's prehistory and of the Carthaginians, but the principal discussion of these subjects will be found in this volume under Minorca and Ibiza respectively, because here is where there is most to be seen of these eras.

The Balearics are today among the most popular tourist centres in the Mediterranean. Tourist popularity leads to development, to the building of hotels, apartments and villas. In my introduction to *Majorca* I wrote: 'in spite of the ever-increasing number of hotels and blocks of flats, the island has not yet been greatly spoiled and is unlikely to be so for many years, if ever.' For this I was strongly taken to task by several critics. Having seen the increased tempo of development in Majorca during the last two or three years, I doubt if I would be quite as optimistic if I were writing that introduction today. Minorca and Ibiza are also being developed; this has been going on for some years. When however one remembers the poverty in Spain before and just after the disastrous civil war of 1936–9, one must be careful not to be overcritical of tourist development, which is by no means unique to Spain. One does nevertheless regret the erection in places of natural beauty of hotels and blocks of apartments especially when quite out of scale with their surroundings. Fortunately, some of the loveliest areas are those where, for technical reasons, it is impracticable or too expensive to build, and both islands have their share of these.

In preparing this book, I would like particularly to thank the Spanish Embassy in London for their help, likewise the Mayors of Mahon and Ciudadela in Minorca, and the Mayor and the Secretary of the Town Hall, Ibiza who allowed me to bring back on loan to London part of the authoritative *Historia de Ibiza* by Canon Isidoro Macabich. I should also like to thank Sr. Don José Manuel Molina of San Antonio Abad. I am especially grateful to Mr. Hugh Gibb whose enthusiasm for the Balearics has been a constant stimulus. I am much indebted to Alexander, my son, for his companionship during one visit to Minorca and for his help in locating various prehistoric monuments. Finally, I would like to record my affectionate gratitude to Clare, my wife, for her continuing encouragement and for her patience and kindness in yet again typing out a manuscript.

Part One

IBIZA

1

The Harbour and Modern Town
of Ibiza

Ibiza, mountainous, pine-covered, lying some 55 miles due east of the Spanish mainland at its nearest point, is the third largest island in the Balearic group. With an area of 229 square miles it is a little over one-sixth of the size of Majorca, which has 1,325 square miles, and is also smaller than Minorca with 290 square miles. Geologically the island is a continuation of the Andalusian Mountains which sweep up through south-eastern Spain as far as Cabo de la Nao, where they disappear into the sea to emerge here at Ibiza and later again at Majorca and Minorca.

The excellent port of Ibiza town in the south-east corner of the island must be one of the oldest in the western Mediterranean, and the ships of the Compañia Trasmediterranea call here regularly from Barcelona, Valencia, Alicante and Palma, capital of Majorca. Their timetables vary according to the season; in the months of July, August and September, the boats from the Peninsular ports arrive here at breakfast time, while the *Mallorca*, which leaves Palma at noon every day, except Sunday, ties up in the harbour at about seven o'clock in the evening. Ibiza also now boasts a fine modern airport and the vastness of the reception area indicates the determination of the Ibicencans to obtain their full share of tourist traffic; its only distinctively Spanish feature on a recent visit was the smell of Spanish tobacco, sweeter and more acrid than the fumes from English and American cigarettes.

It is far more enjoyable to approach a Mediterranean island by sea than by air, especially in summer, and the journey from Palma to Ibiza is particularly attractive. Ibiza can be seen from high up on Majorca's north-west sierra or from the promontory which towers above the entrance to the Puerto d'Andraitx, but it is a little time after leaving Palma before those on board the *Mallorca* become aware

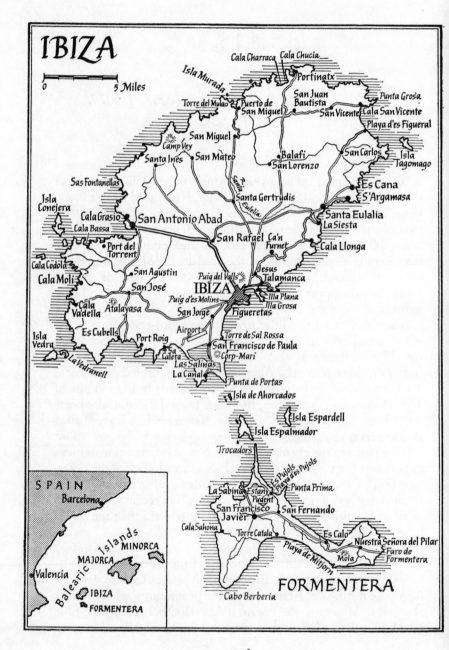

IBIZA

0   5 Miles

Cala Charraca   Cala Chucia

Isla Murada

Portinatx

Torre del Mulao   Puerto de
San Miguel

San Juan
Bautista

Punta Grosa

San Vicente   Cala San Vicente

Playa d'es Figueral

Camp Vey

San Miguel

Santa Ines   San Mateo

Balafi

San Lorenzo

San Carlos

Isla
Tagomago

Sas Fontanellas

Santa Gertrudis

Es Cana

S'Argamasa

Isla
Conejera

Cala Grasio

Cala Bassa

San Antonio Abad

Santa
Eulalia

Santa Eulalia

La Siesta

Port del
Torrent

San Rafael

Ca'n
Furnet

Cala Llonga

Cala Codola

Cala Moli

San Agustin

San José

Puig del Valls

Jesus

Talamanca

IBIZA

Cala
Vadella

Atalayasa

San Jorge

Puig d'es Molins

Illa Plana

Illa Grosa

Figueretas

Isla
Vedra

Es Cubells

Port Roig

Airport

Torre de Sal Rossa

San Francisco de Paula

La Vedranell

Sa
Caleta

Las Salinas

La Canal

Corp-Mari

Punta de Portas

Isla de Ahorcados

Isla Espardell

Isla Espalmador

Trocadors

La Sabina

Estany
Pudent

Es Pujols
Playa d'es Pujols

Punta Prima

San Francisco
Javier

San Fernando

Cala Sahona

Torre Catala

Es Calo

Nuestra Señora del Pilar

Faro de
Formentera

Playa de Mitjorn

Mola

FORMENTERA

Cabo Berberia

S P A I N

Barcelona

Balearic Islands

MINORCA

MAJORCA

Valencia

IBIZA

FORMENTERA

16

of the island of their destination gently rising from the sea. First there is a good lunch to be enjoyed, perhaps a *paella*, followed, as circumstances dictate, by a siesta. After about four hours, by which time the Majorcan sierra is fading into the distance, the steeply wooded hills of northern Ibiza, almost miniature mountain ranges although rarely over 1,000 feet high, begin to take shape, and the cliffs of Tagomago, a magical islet off the north-east coast, become clearer. By this time one is entering an area of islands sufficiently different from Majorca and Minorca to have been given their own distinctive name by the ancients. Diodorus Siculus wrote that Majorca and Minorca, names derived from the Roman *major* (larger) and *minor* (smaller), had together been known as the *Gymnesiae* to the Greeks, because the inhabitants went naked in summer. Ibiza together with Formentera, which lies immediately to the south of Ibiza and is the fourth largest island in the Balearics, were called the *Pityussae* or 'Pine Islands'—a reference to the pines which then covered much of the islands and to some extent still do today.

A more important difference between the *Pityussae* and the more

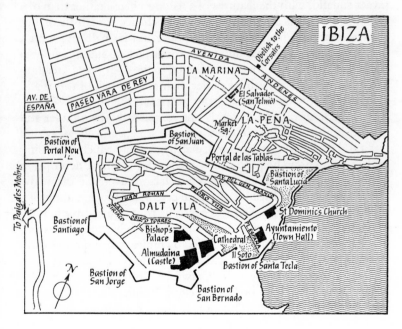

northerly Balearics is that Ibiza was from the middle of the seventh century B.C. one of Carthage's most important colonies. Although the history of the island has since Roman times followed roughly the same pattern as that of Majorca, these first five or six hundred years as part of the Punic Empire have left an elusive yet pervasive feeling both of Africa and the Levant, which is not to be found to the same extent in the Balearic islands to the north-east.

Except for the choice of site, which is particularly Phoenician on Carthaginian—an easily defensible hill or promontory above a harbour which can be used irrespective of wind or season—there is little distinctively Punic or African about present-day Ibiza town with its crowded, bustling port, on which work was started as recently as 1885, or about the older walled town climbing up the hillside beyond. The modernization of the harbour must have proceeded very leisurely, for in 1911 J. E. Crawford Flitch could still write, in *Mediterranean Moods*, that 'the city of Ibiza like many towns upon the Mediterranean, has a deceitful, mirage-like beauty. At a distance it shines like a mount of crystal, but as you approach it the wonder vanishes, and when you enter it you find it disorderly, rather squalid, with the features of a fishing village rather than of a capital. The streets are wide or narrow as chance has left them, but always steep and irregular. Every house has its balcony, with a fluttering array of clothes hung out; fowls pick about hopefully in the gutter; lambs and goats are tethered to the door posts, treading a few wisps of dusty herbage under their feet.' Much of this is still true, except for the lambs and the goats and the squalor. Today, there is little or no dirt which is one reason why the wonder still persists in the older part of the town; the streets and alleyways are clean and the houses well painted, usually in white which is dazzling in the sunshine and helps to justify the tourist brochure description of the island as Isla Blanca or White Island, a phrase originally created by Santiago Rusiñol, the once celebrated Catalan humorist, writer and painter who died as recently as 1931. He became famous in Spain for his description of a Majorca which has long vanished, when the trams of Palma were pulled by mules, when life was care-free and unhurried as it was at the beginning of this century.

One wonders whether Mr. Crawford Flitch met a particular notary who was described by Gaston Vuillier in *The Forgotten Isles*, published in 1896. This notary must have been one of the most extraordinary of his profession. 'A perfect diver and fisher, he would suddenly plunge into the water, and come to the surface holding one fish in his mouth between the teeth and another in each of his hands.' The writer omitted to indicate whether he was in his office clothes or wearing a bathing costume when they went for a stroll together on that remote day in the nineties. Mrs. Mary Stuart Boyd in *Fortunate Isles*, published at about the same time as *Mediterranean Moods*, reported that the local steamship company was able to charge substantially more for taking people away from than bringing them to Ibiza. Today, should such things be possible, the reverse would certainly be the case.

One of the most animated places in town is the quay, with its passenger ships from the Peninsula and Majorca, its ferry boats to neighbouring Formentera, the fishing fleet and the wide variety of boats bringing the island's food and building requirements. Ibiza until fairly recently was largely self-sufficient with regard to food, but the developing tourist programme makes this no longer true. The quay is lined with cafés and bars which, especially in the evening, are thronged with young people pausing here for a drink, for a chat in a bar a little further on, meeting old friends and making new. The waterfront is lined with palm trees. Halfway along, opposite that part of the quay which is reserved for the ships of the Compañía Trasmediterranea, stands an obelisk, which was erected to the memory of the Ibicencan corsairs who so successfully kept the waters round the island clear of raiders from North Africa in the seventeenth century and even more in the eighteenth. The area from here to the eastern end of the waterfront, where the breakwater protecting the inner harbour begins, is known as La Peña, which climbs up towards the Dalt Vila or High (not 'old') Town as far as the bastion of Santa Lucia. The area to the west of the obelisk as far as the end of the harbour, beyond which lies the yacht basin, and up to the bastion of San Juan is called La Marina. Beyond La Marina is the Paseo Vara de Rey, the social and business centre of Ibiza. Further west still is the sprawling modern town which has sprung up only during the last two decades.

The name of La Peña, which means 'rock' in Spanish, refers to the rock on which much of this quarter is built. It is the oldest part of the town lying outside the walls which encircle the Dalt Vila. The spelling of Dalt Vila is a reminder that the spoken language of

Ibiza, as in all the Balearic Islands, is basically Catalan and not Castilian, which is the official language of Spain. There are, moreover, distinctive local variations in the Catalan spoken by Majorcans, Minorcans and Ibicencans.

Once off the waterfront, you start climbing steeply up uneven grey cobbled passageways. Here motorcars are quite out of the question. On to these lanes face little terraced lines of mainly two-storey houses. Their walls are whitewashed and their shutters painted green or, less frequently, a pale golden brown. The rooms on street level are normally paved with dark patternless tiles and often have no window; the open doorway provides sufficient light —and not much is required in summer. Sometimes the ground-floor room is used as a storehouse, perhaps for fishing tackle, in which case there is an outside stairway to the living quarters on the first floor.

These whitewashed cottages were built mainly in the nineteenth century and are the homes of artisans, sailors and fishermen— these last still enjoy a thriving trade as the seas around Ibiza are alive with fish. On Sundays and holidays, the older men and women wear their traditional costume, the men in black suits and berets, and the women in long dark dresses and shawls, with handkerchiefs over their heads, while their hair, plaited into a pigtail and tied with ribbons, hangs down to their waists. This traditional way of dressing was almost universal in the countryside until some twenty years ago. In *The Life and Death of a Spanish Town*, which is about Santa Eulalia on the east coast of the island and was published just before the 1939–45 war, Elliot Paul wrote: 'Most of the Ibicencan women were healthy and strong with eyes alive and a ready smile, and because long centuries of custom had defined their lines of conduct, they were able to be quickly friendly without being sexually sly. Their native costume, which occasional stray painters had made hideous, was becoming to them as good healthy women and was worn by nearly all of them who worked out-of-doors because it covered them from head to foot, several thicknesses, and kept their skin pure white in spite of Ibiza's strong sun.' Perhaps this costume originated with the Muslims from North Africa, where the traditional method of gaining protection from the sun is to cover the body from head to foot.

Other inhabitants of La Peña are the young expatriates who have come from nearly all parts of the world to relax here in this lovely and inexpensive island, not only from Europe and North America, but from other remoter countries such as Ethiopia, South Vietnam and South Korea. Some of them own little bars and restaurants established in the houses facing the waterfront. A proportion live here all the year round and have gained some local acceptance as they stay in their own communities, are law-abiding and have developed several cottage industries for the tourist trade, including leather goods and silverware, whereby they pay their way.

Finally there are the birds of La Peña. The streets and alleyways echo with birdsong, the sweet plaintive calls of canaries, finches and linnets confined in cages so small that they can barely stretch their wings. At least they are out of doors, not hidden away inside, and no doubt adapt themselves to this existence. They are not always alone; on several occasions, three or four tiny cages, each containing one song bird, can be seen nailed close by the entrance to a house or to a first-floor balcony, resplendent with potted plants, flowering creepers and the equally colourful red Buttagas containers.

The area of La Marina is more recently constructed than that of La Peña; some of the land on which it is built was reclaimed from the sea. The houses are taller, the roads wider and metalled. There are one or two small hotels on the waterfront, Ibiza's finest before the arrival of the package tour, and a few simple shops, including a bookshop, in the surrounding streets. Here is the parish church of San Telmo, sometimes called San Salvador, which is attended on Sundays and feast days by the fishermen and sailors of La Peña and La Marina with their wives and families. It is simple and severe in the Baroque style and has been completely restored in recent years. There is little of interest architecturally in this area except, perhaps, for the Plaza del Mercado, or the market square, built in 1872 in an unpretentious, utilitarian Neo-Classical style. The fish market, a separate building, is close by. From here, the main entrance to the Dalt Vila is reached up the ramp to the Portal de las Tablas, hewn out of the great walls built to defend the town during the reign of Philip II.

A few steps further to the west, still under the shadow of the city walls, is the Paseo Vara de Rey, a long gravelled walk, surrounded by one-way streets. It is similar in length to the Borne in Palma, but without the glorious line of trees on each side of the walk, and without the well-laid pavement. Nevertheless, it is the social centre of the town and in the cafés on the north side will be found at appropriate times the leading citizens, a number of expatriates and many more transient visitors, anxious to absorb the local atmosphere. Here, even in winter, it is possible to sit outside, sheltered from the wind, and enjoy the sun. This would not be possible in the Dalt Vila, or in La Peña or La Marina because all the houses face north with their backs to the sun.

In the centre of the Paseo stands a statue to Vara de Rey himself. This was raised by public subscription and personally unveiled by King Alfonso XIII in 1904. It is now so well known that nobody pays it any attention except, perhaps, when the town band, its members replendent in peak caps, plays here under its shadow on a Sunday morning. Vara de Rey, an Ibicencan by birth, was a Spanish general who fought valiantly in the short-lived Spanish–American War in Cuba in 1898, in which he was killed in action. During the years preceding this war, there had been recurrent trouble between the Cubans and the Spanish authorities, which had led to terror and counter-terror. Particularly oppressive was the policy, initiated by General Weyler, of placing all dissident Cubans in concentration camps. General Weyler was a Majorcan and his name is commemorated by a street named after him in Palma. The United States became involved with Cuba because her trade there suffered increasingly on account of unsettled local conditions. Then came the blowing-up of the U.S.S. *Maine* in Havana harbour; as a result war became almost inevitable. The Spanish government in Madrid then offered a far more liberal approach to the Cuban problem than any which had been initiated by her representatives in Cuba and for a time it was hoped that moderation would prevail. President McKinley of the United States was however virtually forced into war by American public opinion, especially when Madrid refused to give Cuba her independence. The war started in May and ended in the August of the same year, by which time Cuba found herself independent and Puerto Rico and the Philippines under the Stars and Stripes.

In the eyes of his countrymen, General Vara de Rey enjoyed a distinguished career and died bravely in the service of Spain. The sculptor, however, seems to have concerned himself in this remarkable work almost entirely with the gallant soldier's animation in battle, from which the quality of Spanish dignity seems to have been largely missed.

To the west of the Paseo begins the post-war town, most of which has come into existence as a result of the tourist boom. This has brought with it so many new jobs—in building, hotel work, transport and food—that there are not enough Ibicencans to fill them. It is therefore no longer necessary for Ibicencans to emigrate overseas to Cuba or Argentina in search of employment, which many were forced to do up to 25 years ago. Work on the land in Ibiza, moreover, has lost its attraction. Employment as a waiter or behind a bar is better paid and less exhausting than agriculture. Only the middle-aged and elderly work on the family farms and it may be that they will be the last generation to do so, although some of the young who work in hotels return home in winter to give much needed help. Unfortunately more and more hotels are remaining open all the year round.

In order to fill the vacancies which an expanding local economy has created, many Spaniards are settling in Ibiza from the Peninsula where there is not always the same prosperity. They come from such areas as Old and New Castile, from Galicia and especially from Andalusia. Because of these immigrants from the Peninsula, together with Ibicencans from elsewhere on the island, there has been a boom in the building of apartment blocks in the heart of the new town. Few of them have any charm of style or detail. These grey concrete blocks stand along streets laid out on the grid system, like any low-grade dormitory area, which would be sad under any circumstances but is particularly so in an island of such individuality and beauty. Even the new church of Santa Cruz is of concrete. A well-designed football ground and a new hospital at the foot of the Puig d'es Molins are also of recent origin.

2

The City Defences and their History

The steeply rising Dalt Vila, basically the mediaeval city of Ibiza, culminates in the cathedral, over which towers its Catalan–Gothic belfry. Also on the crown of the hill is the fortress, once the Moorish Almudaina with its Tower of Homage, but it is largely hidden from view by the cathedral to anyone looking up from the harbour. It is closed to visitors because it is in military occupation. Seen from the Illa (Isla) Plana across the harbour, this great rock with its ancient walls and buildings has both strength and beauty; certainly no city nor harbour in the Balearics can be compared to it.

The main entrance to the Dalt Vila is up the ramp from the Plaza del Mercado and through the Portal de las Tablas, or Gate of the Boards, a reference to the drawbridge which once formed part of it; the wheels on which it was worked are still in position. This was apparently the only entrance to the Dalt Vila when Gaston Vuillier visited the island at the end of the last century. It was here, each morning, that the fruit and vegetable merchants assembled, with their baskets of produce, together with the *aguadores*, or water-carriers, who provided an indispensable service to the inhabitants of the walled town at a time when, except for a few private cisterns, the only water supply came from an old well near the harbour. Today, while water tanks are very useful additions, especially to those houses with gardens, the Dalt Vila has a good, modern water supply. It also has two entrances in addition to the Portal de las Tablas; one is the Portal Nou, or New Gate, at the west end facing in the general direction of the Puig d'es Molins and the other, known as Il Soto, cuts southwards through the ramparts between the cathedral and the Ayuntamiento or Town Hall, but is not much used and is marked on few maps.

The great massive walls which today surround the Dalt Vila

were erected by order of the Emperor Charles V; work started on them in 1554, the year before his abdication. Most of the work was carried out during the reign of Philip II to a design by the distinguished Roman military engineer, Juan Bautista Calvi, who is said to have been responsible for the fortifications of Cadiz, Rosas, Perpignan and Fort St. Philip in Minorca. The sixteenth century was a period when the full impact of the lengthy struggle between Cross and Crescent was felt by those living in the western Mediterranean, in south-east Spain and along the North African coast. Turkey, by capturing Constantinople in 1453, became a naval power because of the need to subdue Christian piracy in the Aegean. The Turkish navy was subsequently used both off the Balkans and in the western Mediterranean against the two wings of Charles V's Empire which extended from Austria and beyond to Spain. The fall in 1492 of the last Muslim principality in Spain, the Kingdom of Granada, was followed by the eviction of all Moors who refused to convert to Christianity. As a result, many Muslims along the North African coast who had been expelled from Spain after being stripped of all their possessions were prepared to go to sea against the Christians, wherever they could be found, in order to gain revenge and booty.

Charles V was at first able to make some headway against Islam and succeeded in seizing Tunis in 1535 from Kheir-ed-Din Barbarossa, perhaps the most formidable of all corsairs in the service of the Sultan Suleiman the Magnificent. Six years later, however, he sustained a disastrous defeat at Algiers; this was the principal port used by Muslim raiders against Spain and the Balearic Islands. To have destroyed this stronghold would have given the hard-pressed Balearics great relief. Unfortunately, Charles's mighty expedition set forth too late in the year and what might well have been a great victory was suddenly overthrown by a violent storm. For the rest of his reign, Charles was to remain on the defensive in the Mediterranean. Not only had he to cope with the Turks and their allies but also with the French. Francis I of France had made an alliance with the Ottoman Empire as the only way of containing Charles V whose power, according to the Grand Vizier, was 'like a flood which, swollen by many a stream and fall, undermines the most solid foundation.' There were a number of reports of French activities in the seas around Ibiza at that time.

It was against this background that Charles V's great defensive system for Ibiza during the sixteenth century was conceived; it consisted of an irregular heptagon with seven bastions, namely those of Santa Tecla, San Bernardo, San Jorge, Santiago, Portal Nou, San Juan and Santa Lucia, each connected to its neighbours by massive walls. The huge blocks of stone of which the fortifications were built were probably hewn out of the hillside on which they stand. The cost must have been prodigious, and although these were the years in which the inflow of treasure from the New World was steadily increasing, every attempt was made to enlist local financial support.

The walls were finally completed in 1585. Philip II never visited them himself, but a report was probably made by Don John of Austria who was able to see the work in progress while cruising in Ibicencan waters in 1575. Above the gateway of the Portal de las Tablas, beneath a finely-carved coat of arms of Aragon and Castile, there is a Latin inscription which gives the date of completion and states that this was in the reign of 'Philip the Second Catholic and most Invincible King of Spain and of the East and West Indies'. Three years later, his 'Invincible Armada' was to be destroyed in the English Channel. The strength of these fortifications was never put to the test in war; the only damage they ever suffered was when a powder magazine blew up in the bastion of Santa Lucia as a result of a flash of lightning in 1730.

The walls we see today are the last, not the first, to have engirdled the Dalt Vila. The Pisan Crusade of 1114, to clear the island of Muslim pirates, had to battle against an elaborate defence system which had been erected by its Muslim rulers, probably using much older walls as a basis for their foundations. The Muslims are said to have made their first contact with Ibiza as early as 698, before they crossed the Straits of Gibraltar into Spain, but it is unlikely that they settled on the island until the end of the eighth century or probably rather later. It was only by the beginning of the tenth century that they were known to be in full control. The Muslim era was not necessarily an unprosperous one for the islanders, whoever they may then have been, but to use the island as a raiding base against Christian shipping, which the Muslims did, was to invite trouble. Muslim piracy was so effective that the Archbishop of Pisa persuaded the Catalans and Pisans to join together in an expedition against Majorca and Ibiza early in the twelfth century. Rome, Lucca, Florence, Siena, Volterra, Pistoia, Lombardy and Sardinia contributed to this fleet, which was blessed by the Pope, Pascal II, who gave it the status of a crusade. In the autumn of 1113, a great concourse of 500 vessels arrived in Barcelona harbour, where they wintered.

In March 1114, an advance party landed in Ibiza but was quickly forced to re-embark by the prompt action of the Muslim cavalry. At the same time, the Muslim ruler of the island sent ambassadors to try and buy off the crusaders—but in vain. On 24th June the main expedition sailed from Barcelona under the command of Raymond, Count of Barcelona, and although it landed without opposition, it found a determined enemy entrenched in the city, protected by three lines of defences.

The siege lasted nearly seven weeks and might have continued very much longer, had it not been for the results obtained by an enormous battering-ram, protected by a high wooden tower, which the crusaders had constructed as soon as they had assessed the situation. This battering-ram was in action incessantly throughout the siege and breached each of the three defence walls in turn. During the battle for the third and last remaining wall, the Muslim second-in-command, Albulanazar, was wounded by a Pisan soldier. After this the Muslim defenders lost heart and resistance finally collapsed on 10th August. Many Christians were released from the dungeons and the booty carried away by the crusaders was said to have been enormous.

But the situation for the Christian expeditionary force was still a precarious one. The Muslim dominion extended right up the Levante coast of the Peninsula from Andalusia to well north of Valencia; a counter-attack could have come from several points on this extended littoral, especially from Denia, from where in fact one was launched a little later. Help could also have come from North Africa or Morocco. The crusaders therefore decided to do no more on Ibiza on that occasion than raze the defences to the ground and then sail for Palma, Majorca. Here, after a fiercely contested siege, they captured the town and released as many as 30,000 prisoners. By this time rumours of an impending counter-attack were even stronger; so after destroying Palma's defences, the crusaders returned to their homes in Catalonia, France and

Italy, leaving the Balearics to their fate. In 1116 both Ibiza and Majorca were occupied by the Almoravide dynasty of Muslims from North Africa and Morocco, a new, fanatical wave of recent converts to Islam. Ibiza had still to wait for more than a century before it was permanently secured for Christianity.

The young James I of Aragon, nicknamed 'the Conqueror', was only 21 when he set sail from Barcelona for Majorca in 1229 as the first step towards reconquering the Balearics which, together with the rest of Spain, had been Christian until the beginning of the eighth century. The siege lasted longer than he anticipated; what with this and the time spent in mopping-up operations, he could not continue to Ibiza in 1230 as originally planned, but had to return to the mainland. In any case the army was no longer in fighting condition. Plague had broken out in Palma, which accounted for many deaths, while many men had gone home, laden with booty and unprepared for further effort.

James was back in Majorca in 1231, for fear of a Muslim counter-attack from North Africa, and again in 1232, when he tricked the Muslim rulers of Minorca into becoming his vassals. His vow, however, given to the *Cortes* at Tarragona in 1228, that he would conquer all the Balearics, was constantly in his mind as shown by the agreement he made with Don Pedro, the Infante, or Crown Prince of Portugal and Nuno Sanchez, Count of Roussillon, to grant Ibiza to them under his suzerainty on condition that they captured the island within a given period. Nothing, however, materialized from this.

Fortunately William de Montgri, the sacristan of Gerona cathedral and Archbishop-elect of Tarragona, who had, like Nuno Sanchez, played a leading role in the invasion of Majorca, asked in December, 1234, for the privilege of conquering Ibiza. James of Aragon tells the story in his *Chronicle*; while it is not absolutely certain that he himself wrote it, its vigorous, straightforward style suggests, in the opinion of H. J. Chaytor, a definite personal authorship. 'De Montgri, Archbishop-elect of Tarragona, Berenguer de Santa Eugenia and his brother came to me at Alcaniz. I was right glad at the election of the former!' De Montgri then asked for Ibiza if he captured it with his own resources. 'Since I myself had not attempted its conquest, and had other things to do at that time, I ought to be willing and glad that he should undertake it, in order that men might say in future times that an Archbishop of Tarragona had conquered the island of Ibiza, which he would hold in my name and for me. I deliberated, and considering it an honour that an Archbishop in my dominions should conquer land from the Saracens and hold it for me, I granted his request.'

De Montgri at once set about preparing his expedition as the agreement was to lapse after ten months, and arranged for a *trabuquet* and a *fonevol*, both of them catapults, to be made. The Infante of Portugal and Nuno Sanchez asked to be associated with the expedition and their offer was accepted. The three agreed in April, 1235 to donate a parish church in honour of God and of the Virgin Mary, to divide the city and castle in equal parts, and to divide the rest of the territory proportionately between them, according to the number of combatants each put into the field. Don Pedro of Portugal and Count Nuno were to receive their territory as feudal vassals of de Montgri to whom they were to swear homage immediately after the conquest of the island.

The successful attack on Ibiza is briskly described in James's *Chronicle*. 'They then went with armoured horses, ships and transports to the harbour of Ibiza, set their camp there, and attacked the town. When they had got their machines ready, the *fonevol*, which was the less powerful, battered the town, and the *trabuquet* the castle. There are three walls to the town, one rising over the other. When they saw that the outside wall of the town was giving way by the battering of the *fonevol*, the besiegers began mining; and when they saw it was time to begin the fight, they tried first petty attacks, and prepared for a general assault. The army was put under arms, and one line of wall was taken; one John Xico of Lerida being the first man who entered the breach. When the Saracens saw they had lost that first wall, they were dreadfully cowed, and parleyed for surrender. In this way was the town taken, and the castle too, for the *trabuquet* had not to throw ten stones against the latter. After Ibiza was taken, there came many times [from Africa] Saracen galleys against it: but by the Grace of God the invaders got there more hurt than did our own people.'

The conquest of Ibiza appears therefore to have been relatively easy, as the siege lasted only a month and six days, starting early in June and ending on 8th August. This may have been because the destruction of the city's walls by the Pisan Crusade had been so thorough that the Muslims, who had their own political problems, had not been able to put them back into sufficiently good repair. Perhaps the defenders had heard of the very rough fate which had befallen many of the defenders of Palma and of the generous terms gained by the Minorcans because they had not attempted resistance. Sufficient is it to marvel at men and horses in heavy armour fighting in the full heat of a Mediterranean summer.

There is, of course, one other possible explanation. According to an old tradition, mentioned in an anonymous history of Ibiza written about 1620, the Muslim ruler had abducted the wife of a brother of his; so angry was the latter that he opened a secret gate through the walls and let in the Christians who were thus enabled to attack the defenders unexpectedly in the rear at the height of the battle. The place in which this Christian brigade had been encamped before the walls, probably close to the Puig d'es Molins, was subsequently known as 'the Field of Treason'. Some historians have preferred to ignore this story because of lack of evidence. Canon Isidor Macabich Llobet, the island's revered historian and archivist, who died in 1973 at the age of ninety, considered that so strong was the tradition that some weight should be given to it. Certainly he had found a reference to 'the Field of Treason' in an earlier document than the anonymous history mentioned above. Canon Macabich was the author of a monumental *Historia de Ibiza*, the work of a long and fruitful lifetime, which is invaluable for an understanding of the island.

After the Reconquest the walls must have been put back into good condition according to the same structural plan as before. They were sound in 1359 when, during the war between Aragon and Castile, a Castilian squadron was sent by Pedro the Cruel to seize Ibiza from his namesake, Pedro IV of Aragon. The Castilians were unsuccessful because William of Llagostera, the Aragonese commander, held out successfully. The King of Aragon subsequently allocated a large sum for strengthening the walls. Ruy Gonzalez Clavijo, sent by Henry III of Castile as ambassador to Tamerlaine, reported in 1403, when sailing past the island, that Ibiza was on a hill adjoining the sea and that there were three rings of walls with people living between them. Little of the walls of this early date survive today, although recent repair work has occasionally revealed Arabic and even Byzantine stonework.

3

Dalt Vila

The Dalt Vila today is a mixture of styles and periods as symbolized by the Portal de las Tablas through which we enter; in addition to the arms of Aragon and Castile and Philip II's inscription over the entrance, two Roman statues, both headless, have been placed in niches on either side of it. Both were found during excavations nearby. The old town has immense character. While many of the buildings which stand beside the steeply winding roads and paths may be eighteenth or even nineteenth century, there is a sufficiently strong atmosphere, coming from a remoter past, that places the Dalt Vila, with its great charm, among those magical places like Toledo and Granada which most powerfully evoke the character of a bygone Spain.

Nearly every visitor who wishes to reach the cathedral at the top of the Dalt Vila will make his way through the Portal de las Tablas, along the Patio de Armas, and then east up the Avenida del Generalissimo Franco, otherwise known as the Paseo de sa Carossa, which is a pleasant tree-lined road backed with ramparts on the north side. After a short distance it swings to the south, climbing briskly all the time, up to the church of St. Dominic (Santo Domingo) and the Ayuntamiento or Town Hall. This is also the road that cars take up to the cathedral, although the number that do so are few on account of the steepness of the route and because there are very few places where two can pass each other. The best way of exploring the town is undoubtedly on foot; many approaches are then available.

The church of St. Dominic, although first started in the sixteenth century, was completely reconstructed in the Baroque manner in the eighteenth century. It has a rich, if unremarkable, interior with a barrel-vaulted ceiling. Outside there are three red-tiled domes of a

pleasing design. Next door, where once stood the San Vicente
Ferrer monastery of the Dominicans, is now the Ayuntamiento,
whose offices are entered off the Plaza España close by. There are
fine views towards Formentera on the seaward side of the building.
The rooms on the upper floor are piled high with documents, some
of them dating back several hundreds of years; some have already
been classified but a considerable quantity are still outstanding.

The road continues steeply uphill towards the cathedral; as
one climbs, it becomes evident that the houses here are not only in
most cases older than those in the lower town, but also grander.
Occasionally the visitor will notice a coat of arms carved over the
entrance of a door, or a carved Renaissance window-frame, or a
round-arched window supported by slender Gothic pillars, as at
the Comasema house. Added dignity is given by the entrance halls
with their stone-slabbed floors and heavy wooden doors leading off.
These mansions belong to the older families of the island, some six
of which can even trace their arrival in Ibiza back to the thirteenth
century; they are sturdy and imposing, with their backs turned on
the outside world. Life inside them is probably concentrated on a
small, delectable garden surrounded by tall stone walls; a palm tree
looming above them may perhaps be the only indication to passers-
by that the garden exists, apart from trailing fronds of wisteria or
bougainvillaea growing over the walls. None of the houses,
however, are on the same grand scale as the town palaces of Palma,
Majorca, or of Ciudadela, Minorca; some have been split up into
several occupations or converted into artists' studios.

The cathedral square lies at the end of the climb. Here is the very
heart of the island's history and character. On the far side is the
great cathedral church, dedicated to St. Mary. To the right is the
Bishop's Palace and beyond it the Almudaina, with its neat sentries
on guard duty. Immediately to the left on arriving in the square
there is an elegant Gothic doorway leading into what was once the
Curia, or mediaeval courthouse, while beyond is the Archaeological
Museum, a long low building of considerable historic interest in
itself which houses many of the relics of the island's past, discovered
during this century.

One of the first acts of the three leaders of the Christian expedition
after their victory in 1235 was to establish, as promised, a parish
church, variously called Santa Maria d'Ibiza (or d'Eivissa in Cata-

1a The old town of Ibiza on its hill seen from the Isla Grosa: the modern
town is on the right

1b Ibiza town with the ramparts and cathedral above

2a The buttresses of Ibiza cathedral with its Catalan-Gothic belfry beyond

2b The church of Santa Eulalia, Ibiza

lan), Neustra Señora de las Nieves (Our Lady of the Snows) and Santa Maria la Mayor (St. Mary the Great). This they probably did by converting to their purpose the Muslim mosque which then stood on the site of the present cathedral. As long as civilized man has been in Ibiza this position seems to have been occupied by a place of worship; the mosque was preceded by a Roman temple, probably dedicated to Mercury, and prior to this a Punic shrine may well have stood here. The existence of a Roman temple here at one time is supported by the discovery, in 1789, of the marble capital of a Corinthian column in use as a curbstone to a well in the Church of the Hospital. This church, dedicated in 1707, has a plain white Baroque west front and stands approximately halfway between the cathedral and the Portal Nou. A plinth was discovered at the same time, whose size indicated that the original temple must have been a magnificent one.

The great cathedral church of warm grey stone which we see today is the result of an extensive rebuilding programme carried out at the beginning of the eighteenth century; Pedro Ferro, a stone-cutter and native of Denia, and Jaime Espinosa, a master architect of Valencia, were given two years to complete the work in 1712. It was not, however, finished until 1728. The original Gothic building was erected in the fourteenth century; the first known reference to the completed church of Santa Maria la Mayor was in 1392 on the occasion of a visit paid to it by a representative of the Archbishop of Tarragona. The original Catalan-Gothic bell-tower, which still dominates the surrounding area, a part of the apse, and the sacristy all date back to the fourteenth century. The sacristy was, however, altered well before the eighteenth century and it is interesting to note that 'the honourable master Antoni Saura, stone-cutter and master craftsman', who was responsible for this work in 1592, bore a good Minorcan name.

The exterior of the church which we see today—dignified, severe, unadorned—while technically in the Baroque manner, has the appearance, when seen in conjunction with the bell-tower, of an earlier period. Most of the stone from the original church must have been used again in the rebuilding. Above the level of the interior side-chapels rise straight, wall-like buttresses, six on the north side and seven on the south. There is no west entrance because the walls of the Almudaina, the last Muslim strongpoint to hold out in the sieges both of 1114 and 1235, rise grimly here just across a narrow passageway from the cathedral. The main entrance, however, a pretty little doorway, faces on to the cathedral square; over it there presides a modern Madonna and Child. Why a rebuilding of the church was necessary is not now apparent. If, however, the original fourteenth-century church was in its turn based on a much older building, in this case probably a mosque, then the repairs necessary by the beginning of the eighteenth century may have been on so large a scale that it was just as cheap to rebuild in a contemporary style. The Ibicencan authorities were never well-off and somewhat isolated from the trends of the day, owing to their distance from the mainland; it is therefore unlikely that they would have had their church reconstructed in the Baroque style merely to be in the fashion. The new church was smaller than its predecessor, as can be seen by the way the mediaeval apse, which was not altered, embraces the narrower body of the new church.

The interior consists of a nave without aisles or transepts unpretentiously rendered in the Baroque manner. The walls are painted a pale cream and decorated with gold and reddish-orange lines. A large chapel stands at the south-west corner of the aisle, close to a memorial, in the middle of the west wall, to those who were killed by Republican extremists in the Spanish Civil War of 1936–39. The interior is light and airy but, unlike the interior and sacristy of the great cathedral of Palma, is not richly endowed, partly because the island is not wealthy, and also perhaps because it was only in 1782 that this, the parish church of Ibiza and Formentera, was elevated to the status of a cathedral.

Because William de Montgri at once became the Archbishop of Tarragona after his victory on Ibiza, there was for centuries a close and special relationship between the Archbishopric and the island. But in those days the distances between the two places must have seemed enormous and the journeys dangerous, especially because of the threat of attack from Saracen corsairs. For this reason, and through pressure of other business, the islanders had on several occasions to wait for twenty years or more before the Archbishop or his representative appeared on the island to confirm those who required it. Phillip II was appreciative of the islanders' request for a bishop of their own, but nothing was achieved because of the difficulty in reaching agreement on what rents should be paid to the proposed see at Ibiza and what to Tarragona. Eventually, in 1782, after continual lobbying over the years by the Ibicencans, Ibiza's parish church became a cathedral, and the new bishopric was granted all the rents which the island had previously sent to Tarragona. The new bishop arrived in 1784 and was conducted to the building, now known as the Bishop's Palace, but which had previously been occupied by the Jesuit order, now expelled from his Spanish dominions by Charles III in 1767.

Even then the future of the see was not assured. In 1851, the bishopric was suppressed and the island included in the see of Majorca until 1927, when it was re-established. Today a suffragan bishop occupies the Bishop's Palace and is responsible for the island to the Bishop of Majorca, who in his turn is subject to the Archbishop of Tarragona.

Although lacking the great variety of treasure to be found in Palma cathedral, a visit to the sacristy is well worthwhile. Among other objects of interest, there are some fine embroideries, and two paintings on wood by Francesch Comes, sometimes called the Inca Master, Inca being the third largest town in Majorca; one is of Santa Tecla and the other of San Antonio Abad. Both of these paintings have in recent years been restored by Arturo Cividini, the distinguished Italian picture restorer. Both were later exhibited at the Lonja, Palma, during the middle and late sixties when the public was given the opportunity of seeing an exhibition of the mediaeval school of Majorcan painting organized by the March Foundation which had commissioned Cividini to restore the works on show. Comes worked in Valencia and Catalonia between 1383 and 1399, before going to Majorca where many fine works of his are to be seen. Whether or not he came to Ibiza is not known, but it was then quite usual for works to be commissioned at a distance.

Perhaps the two most interesting paintings in the cathedral are not in the sacristy but in the rather dark chapel on the south side of the cathedral, next to the entrance to the sacristy. They are of St. James, known in Spain as Santiago, and of St. Matthew, and they are placed one on each side of the altar. They were painted by Valentin Montoliu while he was living at San Mateo in the Maestrazgo, a district which lies inland from Castellon de la Plana, between Valencia and Tarragona. A legal deed, drawn up in San

Mateo in 1468, records that Valentin and his son Luis had delivered five large panels, including the two portraits, to Juan Valls, a merchant who had commissioned them for inclusion in two retables for Ibiza church. The story has been told by Chandler R. Post, the great American scholar of Spanish painting, in his monumental *History of Spanish Painting.* Evidently a brother of Valls was provost of Ibiza church. Montoliu is by no means the greatest of fifteenth-century Spanish painters and the rough, dour severity of his style is more in keeping with the Maestrazgo than with Tarragona where he was born. Nevertheless he is the most important painter of his school and Post draws attention to certain oriental influences at work in, for example, the very rich apparel worn by the two saints. Montoliu's figures appear somewhat awkward—as seen for example in St. James's feet and the thin, powerless hands of both saints—yet both pictures impress by their exotic garments, the elaborate gold tracery of the background and by a certain intensity of expression in the features of the saints.

The Archaeological Museum stands across from the cathedral on the little tree-lined square where, even in the heat of summer, there is usually a slight breeze. The present museum consists of two rooms; one is embellished with Gothic decoration and was originally the Chapel of the Redeemer, while the second was the office of the *Universidad* or Town Council. A reference to the chapel has been found as far back as 1364. Later it became the chapel of a guild of seamen and remained so until 1702, when the *Universidad* acquired it and made the two buildings into one. Some years ago, when restoration work was being carried out on the museum, quantities of bones and funeral remains were discovered underneath the chapel. Here, perhaps, had once been the ossuary of the nearby church. Among the objects found was the very moving wooden image of Christ, the figure thin and bent, which, together with post-Roman coins and some Muslim ceramics, is now to be seen in the museum. The main display space, however, is overwhelmingly devoted to Carthaginian, Greek and Roman relics found on the island, with the exception of those discovered in the Puig d'es Molins just to the south of the town; these are on view in the little museum at the foot of the Puig.

Outside the museum, and looking towards the north, is one of the finest views of the island. Here one can look down over the

Dalt Vila to the fortifications and the harbour beyond. Further still there is the Illa Plana with the pretty bay of Talamanca behind, and then the low hills which rim the horizon from north to west, guarding the small-holdings and the slowly spreading suburbs and factory areas. Fortunately these developments have all been painted white in keeping with the island's traditions.

❧ 4 ❧

Salt and the Saracens

In 1232, after the capture of Majorca, James I of Aragon granted a Charter of Privileges to all the Balearic Islands, including Ibiza which was still under Muslim control. This in effect acknowledged the rights not only of the nobility and gentry but also of the merchants, the artisan and agricultural classes, all of whom were to be represented in the *Universidad*. In Italy, Germany and elsewhere in Europe, the new classes thrown up by the development of production and commerce were having to fight hard, often bitterly, for these privileges of representation in local government, but in the Balearics they were gained as a reward for conquest. Throughout the island's history, there are frequent references to the island's pride in these rights and their insistence, whenever possible, on proper respect being shown to them.

Every spring saw the election take place of the various dignitaries who advised on or who took part in the running of the island's administration, which included not only Ibiza but Formentera as well. Obsolete forms of justice were dispensed with: thus trial by ordeal, whereby the accused was made to undergo certain physical endurance tests to discover whether he was guilty or innocent, was no longer used. No judicial agent was allowed to enter a house, ship, mill or any other place of residence or business except in the presence of two men of good repute. These privileges were generally well in advance of the age. Ibicencans liked to think in those days of their island as a city-state, like for example, Amalfi, both because it was a fortified city by the sea and because of its social and economic structure.

The subsequent history of the island after 1235 was in turn turbulent and peaceful. Its remoteness out in the Mediterranean, away from the centres of power in Aragon and with its lines of communication constantly threatened by Saracen corsairs, must have encouraged the local royal or ecclesiastical representative to overstep his power on occasion. All too often the islanders' only option was to give way, especially when they were not fully in the picture about shifts in political power. In 1286, Alfonso III of Aragon chased his uncle, James II of Majorca, out of Majorca and sent representatives to Ibiza demanding their allegiance. The Ibicencans said they would be prepared to give their allegiance to Alfonso in person, who accordingly arrived with four armed galleys to receive their homage.

In addition to extortionate officials, quarrels arose between church and state about feudal rights and dues, in the course of which the church, represented by the Archbishop of Tarragona, would make vigorous use of the threat of excommunication when it thought necessary, although it did not always achieve the intended result. After Alfonso III's death, James II of Majorca, now returned to his island kingdom, appointed Bernard Zafortesa as Governor of Ibiza. Zafortesa apparently saw fit to seize the ecclesiastical taxes of Formentera. He was excommunicated by the Archbishop, and consequently invaded the church of St. Mary with his troops, disrupting the services.

In 1343, the Kingdom of Majorca to which the Balearic Islands belonged, came to an end. Peter IV of Aragon invaded Majorca in that year and put James III of Majorca to flight. He then declared all the Balearic Islands incorporated into the Kingdom of Aragon, which he was entitled to do as the Kings of Majorca were in vassalage to the Kings of Aragon. In return for the islanders' homage, Peter granted them valuable tax concessions, which were received with much gratitude. There was good reason why the monarchs of the period were anxious to retain the goodwill of the Ibicencans. The islanders owned very valuable salt pans which was their basic source of revenue, and the subsequent history of the island is much involved both with the salt supplies and with continuing harassment from the Saracen corsairs.

The salt pans at Las Salinas in the south-eastern corner of the island had first been developed by the Carthaginians. Today, some forty ponds, once a small lake, make up the salt-producing area and the product is still important for the island's economy, although not to the same degree since the rise of tourism. At all periods of

Ibiza's history there are references to the salt pans. Al-Makhari, the Arab geographer, writing during the Muslim domination, reported that Ibiza provided much of Africa, presumably meaning its Mediterranean littoral, with salt and firewood. After the Reconquest, the salt pans were further exploited. The islanders received their salt free of payment and the local authorities frequently had to pay their royal dues in it because money was in such short supply, often embarrassingly so. When, for example, the great defences were being built during the reign of Philip II, Ibiza paid its share in salt.

Ibicencan salt was particularly valued for two reasons; one was its quality, and the other because supplies were easily accessible to the shipping routes of the western Mediterranean. So marketable was the salt that one gets the impression that during the latter half of the sixteenth century and in the early seventeenth century, agriculture was somewhat neglected; certainly there was then a great shortage of wheat and other provisions. Alternatively, and more likely, the growth of population may have outpaced available supplies; this was certainly true of Spain during the sixteenth century. In 1585, whatever the cause, supplies of grain were so reduced that even the amount that was put on one side for the spring sowing was consumed. So desperate were the local authorities that a cargo of biscuit intended for the King was seized in the harbour. On one occasion, when the island's own supply-ships had been wrecked, the unexpected arrival of two other ships with provisions seemed so miraculous that the Archbishop of Tarragona was asked to authorize a special day of thanksgiving.

During these food shortages, which seem to have been general, the prize often went to the strongest. In 1628, another year when there was a terrible dearth, three ships in Ibiza harbour, two Flemish and one English, were about to discharge their cargo of wheat when they were seized by two great warships under the command of the Marques de Villafranca. He impounded their cargo for his own use and, in spite of the strongest representations by the local authorities, calmly indicated that he considered his need greater than that of Ibiza and proceeded to sail away with the lot. Many attempts were made to obtain redress for this seizure from the crown, and it was made clear how difficult it was to develop foreign trade, especially the export of salt, if such behaviour was allowed to happen. It is unlikely, however, that Ibiza was ever paid compensation.

During the sixteenth century and afterwards, exports of Ibicencan salt not only reached all parts of the Spanish Levante coast but the Tyrrhenian coast of Italy as well, where it augmented supplies from Trapani in Sicily. The shipping of this period, like the Phoenician and Greek sailors of the ancient world, preferred to hug the coastline and not to sail out of sight of land. There was however a well-accepted short route from Spain to Italy via the Balearics—Ibiza, Majorca, Minorca and Sardinia. This route, according to Fernand Braudel in *The Mediterranean World in the Age of Philip the Second,* was known as 'sailing the islands'; it was equally well known in ancient days. The purchasers of Ibicencan salt were the great Italian mercantile companies which had developed special bulk carriers for salt and grain. These were larger ships than those used by the coastal traders, who were primarily interested in carrying a mixed cargo up and down a given coastline.

The bulk carriers would arrive with grain, perhaps from Sicily, which in the sixteenth century, as in Greek and Roman days, was one of the principal grain-growing centres of the Mediterranean, and depart with salt. At one stage of the island's history, the local authorities made it a condition that ships coming to pick up salt must arrive laden with grain. Further illustration of the importance of Ibicencan salt in that corner of the Mediterranean is again given by the establishment of a tunny fishery on the island by a Valencian in 1634.

Work at Las Salinas must always have been hard and disagreeable, especially in summer when the salt crystals can produce a dazzling glare for those toiling in the pans. Workers were therefore introduced from overseas, especially, of course, slaves taken from Saracen ships or from North Africa. There may, in addition, have been a few *Moriscos*, Muslims born in Christian Spain, who had not left during the final expulsions in 1609–10, together with local criminals.

Slaves were a normal part of a rich man's entourage in Catholic Spain in the sixteenth and seventeenth centuries, as in some other highly civilized parts of the world. They worked on the land and in the household and were treated very differently to those who were committed to the galleys. In many cases they were probably treated

too leniently, at least in the opinion of the Ibicencan local authorities who appointed a special officer to see that owners kept a
vigilant eye on their slaves. The constant fear was that these slaves
might, as Muslims, act as guides to Saracen corsairs in raids against
the locality. There were strict regulations about what a Moorish
slave was forbidden to do—he could not rent a house, nor possess
a boat, nor fish off-shore, nor gamble with dice or in any other way.
The penalties—so many strokes of the lash or fines and other
punishments—were clearly set out.

Canon Macabich recounts an unusual story of a slightly earlier
date. In 1502 the Muslims of Castile were offered either conversion
to Christianity or expulsion from Spain; this was the first of several
moves to rid Spain of Islam. A Moor captured by Ibicencans was
put to the oars and, extraordinary to relate, became a convinced and
devoted Christian. Then the Ibicencan galley in which he rowed
came to grief on the Barbary Coast and the Moor found himself
once more among his own people. Instead of being happy with this
change of fortune he longed to return to Ibiza and his adopted
religion. He was eventually exchanged for another Moor, returned
to his beloved island and served as a beadle in the church of St.
Mary on feast days.

The other non-Christian race in Spain, the Jews, who had established themselves in the Peninsula at the time of the Roman Empire,
appeared to have been but few in number in Ibiza and of little
importance. Certainly there is no record on the island of the sort
of terrible persecution which they suffered in Palma, Majorca, and
elsewhere in Spain in 1391, or of the mass conversion which took
place in Majorca in 1435. It is probable that a conversion of sorts
took place before 1410 for in that year we know that the Archbishop
of Tarragona sent a representative to Ibiza to tighten up the
church attendance of the community, which had obviously become
rather lax. These *Conversos*, or Jews who had adopted Christianity,
apparently included some who made a point of glorying in their
new faith, but attended divine service only about once a year.
Quite obviously the converted Jews were carefully watched and
the Archbishop's representative had pointed out to him those who
were sincere in their new religion and those who might have doubts
and might easily be encouraged to revive the ancient rituals of the
Mosaic Law.

The other major problem which affected the lives of the islanders for several generations, and especially from the end of the fifteenth until well into the seventeenth century was that the Muslim corsairs from Africa. During this period Ibiza was under almost continuous attack. The signal for the rapid development of naval action between the Cross and the Crescent was the fall in 1492 of Granada, the last independent Muslim state on Spanish soil. Canon Macabich has given details of a diary, kept by a local official in Ibiza, for the year 1493, of which the following is an extract:

4th April—three ships armed to attack the Moorish boats at San Antonio.

12th April—new armament ready to face the Moorish ships at La Britja.

May—sent a boat to Majorca with news about the Moors.

8th June—advised the villages about the presence of the Moorish flotilla.

9th June—fresh intelligence brought by a boat who had discovered Moorish ships off Tagomago.

11th June—informed Santa Eulalia that no one should be allowed to land from Majorca because of the epidemic there.

18th June—informed villages about the Moorish boat seen off Formentera. Received news of two Moorish ships off the coast.

19th June—informed villages about two Moorish ships seen off Formentera.

26th June—fresh information received at night about a Moorish ship off an island to the west of San Antonio.

2nd July—told villages of two Moorish ships off Cabo de Juan where they captured Antonio Langer.

5th July—told villages of fire signals from the tower at Formentera. Sent ship to Formentera in search of news. A Genoese boat landed garments on the beach in order to burn them for fear of contagion.

9th July—informed Santa Eulalia about Moorish boat, which had arrived off Punta d'en Mari. Informed San Antonio, Las Salinas and Balanzat about Moorish ships which had arrived at Punta d'en Planells.

10th July—advised villages about cannon fire heard at El Vedra.

21st July—informed villages of boats arriving from Majorca with fugitives from the epidemic.

22nd July—armed two ships to go to El Vedra and the Isla Conejera because of the Moorish craft there.

29th August—warned the tower guards of the arrival of a Moorish galley in the area.

15th September—instructed the commander of Santa Eulalia district to try and gain possession of one of the Ragusan galleons. Published an announcement that a truce had been agreed with Genoa and Nice.

22nd November—Governor visits Santa Eulalia because of the presence there of several Moorish ships.

2nd December—informed villages about six Turkish galleys.

The records kept during this period of Ibiza's history are rich in detail. They tell not only of the dangers that came from the sea, but also of the condition of the flagstones in the streets, and of the repairs carried out to the municipal building, to the watch towers overlooking the sea and to the castle. Details of the cost of the mace-bearer's cloak are given, as well as the design of the hoods (in fine purple and black cloth) for the local justices and of the silver staffs used in the parish church. We find references to the gathering of firewood, not only for the town's ovens but for signalling purposes; to the erection of town mills, powered by donkeys, capable of grinding flour for the town's bread in event of a siege; to the replenishment of the town arsenal and to the ordering of materials from which bombs could be manufactured. In those days, Genoa was a great armaments centre and we find the Ibicencan authorities placing orders there early in the sixteenth century for guns and bombs. As one of the great merchant states of the Mediterranean, Genoa had representatives stationed at various trading points throughout the inland sea, including North Africa; these representatives proved a useful source of intelligence about Muslim plans and activities.

One of Ibiza's duties was to keep Majorca informed when danger loomed. It was a continuing function, bearing in mind the island's greater propinquity to North Africa. In 1561, for example, a ship was sent post haste to Majorca to report that 23 Muslim warships had put in either to one of Ibiza's remoter bays or to a nearby island, probably Formentera, to take on water. This was the year when Soller in Majorca was attacked in strength by 1,700 Moors, carried there in 22 galleons under the command of Ochiali, one of the most famous of Saracen corsairs. Thanks, however, to the warning received from Ibiza, the militia were alerted in strength and the raiders defeated with heavy losses. Soller still celebrates this victory early each May.

The corsairs were not the only source of danger. In 1518, Hugo of Moncada, who bore a proud Catalan name remembered espec-ially in connection with James I of Aragon's invasion of Majorca in 1229, was, as Viceroy of Sicily, in command of an expedition to seize the Argel, the fortress which commands Algiers. Suddenly, however, a tempest arose which scattered his fleet and many of his ships were lost. He put into Ibiza harbour to refit. His troops, while there, mutinied because they had not been paid and did damage to the town amounting to over 28,000 ducats, a sum which still had not been settled by the crown a century later.

In 1521 another unexpected disaster occurred. There had been increasing popular unrest throughout Spain because of the dependence of the young King Charles I of Aragon and Castile upon foreign advisers and officials. This unrest increased further after 1518, the year in which he was elected Holy Roman Emperor, as Charles V, at vast expense, because of the greatly increased taxation which was needed to maintain the Empire. The forms in which this unrest expressed itself varied in different parts of the country. In Castile, protest was at first moderate, but in Valencia, where the plague had broken out in 1519, the reaction was very much more extreme. The *Germania*, or brotherhood, which deve-loped there, became a violently radical social movement, as well as an expression of protest against a frequently absent monarch. This infection of ideas spread to Majorca, where a *Germania* was likewise established by the burgesses and artisans who seized control of Palma from the royal Governor, Don Miguel de Gurrea, who was forced to flee to Ibiza.

The smaller island remained apparently unaffected, perhaps because the little community was used to standing together when danger threatened and because there were no great territorial magnates on Ibiza as in Majorca and on the Peninsula. The Ibicen-cans may also have been alarmed at reports of excesses carried out in Majorca, where many of the nobility were slain. These reports would have reached Ibiza through fugitives and perhaps from the crew of one of the naval vessels belonging to the Majorcan *Germania* which was blown by a storm into Ibiza harbour. So eloquently did Don Miguel de Gurrea address the crew of this vessel that they decided not to return to Majorca. Several naval craft with troops were then sent to Ibiza by the *Germania* to demand the release of the defecting ship. When the Ibicencans refused, the commander of the Majorcan flotilla ordered his troops ashore with the aim of capturing the town. They were however beaten back with some losses and forced to return empty-handed to Majorca.

The first half of the seventeenth century saw the island still struggling to maintain its rights, still trying to cope with food shortages, and still fighting against corruption. The Saracen corsairs kept up their pressure and then, in 1662, came the plague. Strict regulations were issued with regard to local travel. Cemeteries for the dead were made just outside the city walls and on the Puig d'es Molins. The church of Our Lady of Jesus, about a mile and a half outside the town on the way to Santa Eulalia via the Cala Llonga, was turned into a hospital for the afflicted; this had originally been a monastery, but had been abandoned by the monks, who had moved into Ibiza town for safety, away from the threat of Muslim raids. Several slaves were persuaded, in return for a considerable reward, to transport the sick, bury the dead and dispose of their garments. Altogether some 711 died in the epidemic, including two doctors; this must have been a heavy loss to the community as the island's total population, according to a count taken in 1669, amounted to no more than 9,600.

❦ 5 ❦

The Later History of Ibiza

In the struggle with Islam and the corsairs, the turning point undoubtedly came in 1571, when the Turks suffered a decisive defeat at the hands of a combined Christian fleet under the command of Don John of Austria at Lepanto, off the Gulf of Corinth. From then onwards the Turkish fleet was increasingly on the defensive.

To the western Mediterranean, this merely meant that Muslim expeditions fitted out against the Balearics during the seventeenth century were no longer military and naval undertakings against territories lost to the Christians during the Reconquest; their resources no longer allowed for this. There was, however, a plentiful supply of merchantmen on which the corsairs could prey, and remoter ports and isolated coastal villages to sack. The price of Christian slaves in the markets of North Africa and Istanbul still made their capture a profitable venture.

By the middle of the eighteenth century, however, the initiative had passed to the Christian forces, and the long galleys of the Dey of Algiers operated very largely within his own territorial waters, partly because of the waxing strength of Spanish, and particularly of Ibicencan, privateers and partly because of the growing number of European warships in the Mediterranean to which, at the end of the century, could be added those of the United States navy. The Napoleonic Wars probably prolonged the life of the Barbary pirates operating off North Africa since the naval powers were for that period otherwise employed, but as soon as peace had been concluded after Waterloo, brisk measures were taken against them. In 1816, an Anglo–Dutch fleet under the command of Lord Exmouth bombarded Algiers and destroyed its fleet. Fourteen years later, the French occupied Algiers. It was only then that the inhabitants of the Balearics and especially Ibiza, only 160 miles away, at last felt secure from the Muslim threat from the sea.

The beginning of the eighteenth century brought fresh problems to Spain, including Ibiza, and to many parts of Europe. The death in 1700 of Charles II, the last degenerate descendant of the Spanish Habsburg dynasty, heralded the outbreak of the War of the Spanish Succession which was to last until 1713, when the Treaty of Utrecht marked the victory of the French Bourbon candidate for the crown and the severance from Spain of Flanders, Milan and Naples. Charles II, having no offspring, had nominated as his successor Philip Duke of Anjou and grandson of Louis XIV of France, who was still vigorously alive. This decision was hotly contested by the Archduke Charles of Austria with support from Britain and Holland, who both feared that the combined strength of France and Spain could throw the balance of Europe against them. The British fleet was soon active in the Mediterranean and, in 1706, a squadron of 28 ships under the command of Sir John Leake, and bearing representatives of the Austrian claimant, appeared off Ibiza. The island was therefore compelled to give support to the Archduke, as Valencia and Catalonia had already done, and as Majorca, Sir John's next port of call, was also to do. Majorca was in fact to hold out the longest of any part of Spain against the Bourbons, even after Catalonia had been beaten into submission.

Ibiza does not seem to have suffered directly from this dynastic struggle except in one important respect, which related to the ownership of the ever-valuable salt pans. In 1710, an order had come from the Archduke Charles, who acted as king in those parts of Spain where his writ was accepted, placing the salt pans in the charge of one Visconti who had gained a contract from him on promising to produce better results than the Ibicencans. Admittedly, the salt pans were not in good shape at the time; the connecting paths between them needed repair and the pans themselves were silted up with mud as a result of a storm. The decision, however, to remove control of Las Salinas from the local authorities and place it in foreign hands produced the greatest possible indignation. The situation was not changed by the Archduke's renunciation of his claim to the Spanish throne when he inherited the Imperial crown on his brother's death. The unrest on the island

3a The fortress church of San Jorge, Ibiza

3b A fig tree on Formentera

4a Sa Torreta *taula*, Minorca

4b The Cales Coves, Minorca: the cliffs are honeycombed with prehistoric caves

continued, and there were rumours of a conspiracy to invite Britain to become the occupying power.

The question of the ownership of Las Salinas continued to be debated for many more years until a decision was made in 1734 by King Philip V; it was not, however, a decision that proved to be final. Philip refused to recognize the islanders' privileges, saying that these had lapsed when they undertook to support the Archduke Charles during the War of the Spanish Succession. He agreed, however, out of charity to pay an annual rent of 26,000 pesos 'in perpetua'—the payment, according to one account, to be in salt. One condition of this agreement was that the islanders must be prepared to bear arms when called upon to do so. It is probably for this reason that we find Ibiza, during the Seven Years War (1756–63), offering to equip a troop of 26 men, commanded by a lieutenant, two sergeants and two corporals.

Difficulties over the salt pans arose again in the nineteenth century, when Napoleon seized the throne of Spain. From this time onwards, the annual rent ceased to be paid to the islanders. When the first Carlist War, an internal dynastic struggle for the crown, broke out in 1833, the 'liberal' government in Madrid accepted the obligation, as laid down by Philip V, to pay rent for Las Salinas but was never able to do so through lack of funds. Eventually, the salt pans were sold in 1871 to a private company, which also acquired the smaller but nevertheless valuable salt pans on Formentera. Those who were most inconvenienced were, of course, the islanders. Until payment lapsed during the Napoleonic Wars, they had always received their salt free of charge, and ever since they have had to pay for it.

While Ibiza suffered the loss of the salt pans as a victim of international intrigue and war, there was one field of activity in the eighteenth century, already briefly mentioned above, in which the island vigorously took the offensive. Ibicencan privateers first came into prominence after the destruction of the Turkish fleet at Lepanto; by the eighteenth century and in the early years of the nineteenth, they were extremely active. Their spirit and achievements are commemorated with pride by the obelisk which stands halfway along the waterfront of Ibiza town.

There were three reasons, according to Canon Macabich, why Ibicencan privateering flourished; there was first the desire to protect Ibiza and the surrounding islanders from the Saracen raiders, then there was the need to capture slaves for work on the land and, thirdly, the spirit of adventure. Also, no doubt, there was the booty which was the reward of such enterprises. The islanders, incidentally, built their own ships, an activity which continued until very recently, and supplied the Majorcans as well. Today, the Ibicencans go to Majorca for their requirements.

One of the earliest privateers on record was Pedro Bernat, who sometime about 1359 was authorized to arm a ship he had captured. Afterwards he became the terror of the Galician coast, having two boats under command. Canon Macabich mentioned a number of exploits by Ibicencans during the eighteenth century, including the following. In 1711, Bernard Ramon captured two ships off Sicily, and in 1716 seized a cargo of wine from a French ship. In 1714, Augustin Barcelo was responsible for the capture of a French cargo boat off Africa. The distinction between pirate and privateer must at times have been very narrow. In 1739, four Ibicencan armed vessels under the command of Mateo Calvet captured off Majorca two Algerian corsairs, which had a Catalan prize in tow. In 1755, Vicente Ferrer, together with José Prats, captured two Moorish ships off the Barbary coast.

One of the most impressive feats carried out by an Ibicencan privateer was the capture in 1806 in full view of the town of a much larger privateer sailing under the British flag. The hero of the hour was Antonio Riquer, who was much respected for his various exploits on the high seas. On this particular occasion, his own boat was being caulked on one of the islets between Ibiza and Formentera when the British privateer *Felicity* with fourteen guns and a complement of some 65 men came into view; its commander was one Miguel or Michael Novelli, whose name does not seem to be of English origin. The appearance of the *Felicity* so close in towards Ibiza was taken as a challenge by Riquer. He therefore had his boat, the *San Antonio*, put to sea with all possible speed and quickly manned. Then he floated gently towards the *Felicity* with a slight following wind. Having got within range, Riquer gave orders to fire, but all eight of his cannon missed their target. The *Felicity* fired in turn and inflicted some damage on the *San Antonio*, killing five of the crew, including Riquer's father, who had insisted on being included. Riquer then ordered his crew to bring his vessel

as close to the enemy as possible and bombarded the *Felicity* with
bottles of gunpowder which exploded and set fire to her stern.
The men of the *Felicity* were therefore compelled to retreat to the
bow, where they were hemmed in by the Ibicencans, who had by
this time clambered on board. In the fighting which followed,
eleven of the British ship's crew were killed and 25 injured. The
Felicity was thus forced to strike her colours. This must have been
a thrilling spectacle for the inhabitants of the town. There is
also a reference to the capture in 1808 of a Catalan ship from the
British by Don Carlos Tur of Formentera, but details are lacking.
After this date Britain and Spain co-operated for the rest of the
Napoleonic Wars against the common enemy.

With the fading of the threat from North Africa and the end of
privateering, Ibiza entered an era of tranquillity. Admittedly there
was a Carlist conspiracy in 1835, as there was in Majorca, but it was
unsuccessful and two of the plotters, who had been sent to Majorca
for trial, were executed there. During the rest of the century, little
of note occurred. In 1836, the first printing press was established.
In 1852, the first steam mailboat was brought into service between
Ibiza and Majorca and, from 1858 onwards, was placed on a regular
weekly basis. In 1862, a daily postal delivery was started on horse-
back to the interior of the island.

At the beginning of the present century, Ibiza was remote and
unknown. It had its own language, Ibicencan, a distinctive variation of Catalan. It had, and still has, a unique species of dog,
dissimilar from any other breed to be found in Europe, but which
can be seen depicted on the tombs of ancient Egypt, and may well
have been brought here by the Carthaginians. The islanders had
their distinctive folk costume, which was then universally worn,
and practised courting customs of a singularly aggressive nature.
A girl could have a number of suitors who would be allowed to
visit her on certain evenings. Each suitor was allowed some fifteen
minutes of her company in the presence of her parents. If a suitor
overstayed his time, however much encouraged by the girl, he
was liable to become involved in a vendetta with the other suitors
which could even end in death. Firearms were freely used on these
occasions—to announce a suitor's arrival, to warn whoever was
with the girl that his time was up—and were even fired into the
ground near the girl's feet, when leaving church, to attract her

attention. Such customs continued in the interior of the island at least until the second decade of this century. Many of them have now disappeared. Yet, within living memory, the lamps in Ibiza town were only lit when there was a bright moon; there was no point in lighting them on a cloudy night as nobody would bother to go out under such conditions.

6

Ibiza from its Earliest Days

From the back of the Dalt Vila there rises a second limestone hill which runs southwards and down into the spreading suburb and seaside resort of Figueretas. On top of the hill stand the round towers of several windmills which give it the name of Puig d'es Molins or, in English, Windmill Hill or Mill Hill. Much of its eastern and southern slopes are now covered with hotels, villas and apartment blocks, but there is sufficient of the hillside not built over to indicate the importance of the site to the archaeologist. For the Puig d'es Molins is a vast cemetery which was in use for nearly a thousand years, from the time when the first Carthaginians started creating their distinctive burial chambers in the rocky hillside.

The traditional date for the foundation of the Carthaginian settlement on Ibiza, handed down to us by Diodorus Siculus, is 654 B.C. Whether Ibiza was inhabited before the Punic arrival is not known, but no remains of the Neolithic or Early Bronze Ages have yet been found. It is certainly surprising that the Neolithic peoples who settled in Minorca and Majorca from somewhere to the east, perhaps from Sardinia or the Italian mainland, probably between the fourth and second millennia B.C., did not reach Ibiza, as the island can clearly be seen from many vantage points in Majorca. Nevertheless there are no traces here of the stone buildings of the *Talayot* culture which are scattered widely over the two largest of the Balearic Islands. There are some strange drawings or graffiti on the walls of a cave at Sas Fontanellas on the west coast, north of San Antonio Abad, which were at one time thought possibly to be the work of people who lived here before the Carthaginians, but opinion is now generally against this interpretation. Again, there is no evidence to support the supposition that Chaldaeans and Egyptians may have been the first settlers here in conjunction with the Phoenicians, in spite of the strong cultural influences of all three civilizations on the Punic arts and crafts as shown in the archaeological discoveries made at the Puig d'es Molins and elsewhere in Ibiza.

The Phoenicians were trading in southern Spain from about 1100 B.C. or even earlier, and had founded an important commercial centre at Gades, now Cadiz. Both they and the Greeks, who arrived several centuries later, were active there because of the metals which could be mined or acquired in that area, especially Spanish silver and tin from Cornwall. The Phoenicians, operating from the twin ports of Tyre and Sidon, had emerged as a vigorous independent power after the decline of the Mycenaeans in the eastern Mediterranean. Their arts and crafts reflected their contacts with Egypt and the peoples of Asia Minor. Because of their involvement in commerce and navigation, they became the connecting link between East and West. One of their greatest achievements was the spreading of a handwritten script (out of which the Greeks later developed the alphabet), thus opening up horizons without end to the human mind. The decline of Tyre and Sidon as a great power did not mean the end of Phoenician culture as this and their trading complex in the central and western Mediterranean was inherited by Carthage, their daughter city founded in 814 B.C. on the North African coast near the site of modern Tunis.

Both the Phoenicians and the Greeks must have known Ibiza because of its strategic position on the more northerly of the two main seaways from southern Spain to the Levant, on the inter-island route which went eastwards past Minorca to the southern tip of Sardinia, then down to Sicily and on to the eastern Mediterranean. The other route followed the North African coast past Carthage. A Greek settlement was established at some time at Hemeroskopeion, on the Spanish mainland near Cabo de la Nao, facing Ibiza at the western end of this inter-island route. It seems odd that no attempt was made to set up a station on Ibiza itself. There is no conclusive proof that the Greeks were ever here, although it is just possible that the settlement at Puig del Valls, which lies to the east of the Ibiza–San Rafael road a little over one mile north of the capital, may have been Greek, judging by the many Greek objects found here when the site was excavated in 1906; a great many Phoenician relics were also unearthed. If the

Greeks settled here for a time, they may have been ejected by the Carthaginians.

The establishment of a colony in Ibiza, which they called Ebusus or Ibusim, is the first recorded action by Carthage. It was a highly significant step because of the strategic importance of the island to the approaches to the Peninsula. With the possession of Ibiza, as well as Cadiz, southern Sardinia and the western tip of Sicily, Carthage was assured of a most powerful defensive network guarding the seas around her. The Greeks by this time were less active in southern Spain and concentrating more on the northern Mediterranean. Greeks from Phocaea, near modern Smyrna, built Massilia, or Marseilles, close to the mouth of the Rhône in 600 B.C. They next set up a colony at Alalia in Corsica in about 560 B.C. and ten years later established a base at Emporion, now called Ampurias, on the Catalan Costa Brava. Was this an attempt to strengthen ties once more with southern Spain? We only know that the Carthaginians found it politic at this time to reach an understanding with the Etruscans in Italy and that their combined fleet defeated the Phocaeans, who had provoked the battle, off Alalia in 535 B.C. From this time until the outbreak of the Second Punic War towards the end of the third century B.C., when Carthage was destroyed by Rome, there appears to have been peace in the Balearics.

The original Carthaginian settlement in Ibiza may have been on the Illa Plana, now joined to the main island on the north side of Ibiza harbour and much developed with hotels and villas, but then an islet as its name implies. Several very primitive figurines, dating from the seventh century B.C. and now to be seen in the Archaeological Museum in the cathedral square, have been discovered here, together with the foundations of a small temple, perhaps dedicated to Eshmun, a deity worshipped by the Carthaginians, who has been linked with Aesclepius, the Greek god of healing. Traces of primitive buildings have also been found on the Illa, used perhaps for the manufacture of purple dye, as a large heap of murex shells, which we know were used in this process, were unearthed nearby. It is possible, too, that they were used for fish-curing, as this was another industry the Carthaginians inherited from Tyre and Sidon. Salt is a basic requirement for curing fish and they must have quickly appreciated the value of the local salt pans at Las Salinas. They would also have been attracted by the lead mines, a little to the south of San Carlos, which have been in fairly continuous use over the centuries, although now no more.

The expansion of the colony would inevitably have led the Carthaginians to settle on the south side of Ibiza harbour, where the island's capital has always been, for here they would have had an excellent base for the defence of what is now the Dalt Vila and facilities for burying their dead in their traditional way. Like other Semitic peoples, the Carthaginians were profoundly religious and devoted not only to their ancestors but also to all the beliefs and traditions relating to life beyond the grave. The city of the dead was therefore as important to them as the city of the living, which would whenever possible be sited close to a hill, in this case the Puig d'es Molins, so that their graves could be dug with the maximum security and secrecy.

A walk over the Puig d'es Molins sadly reveals how unsuccessful the Carthaginians were in their attempts to keep their tombs intact. Every one of the excavations visible in the hillside are Punic graves, which have been rifled in ancient or more recent days. These graves are filled with debris, litter and weeds, in spite of the fact that the Puig has been declared a national monument. Their layout, however, can be clearly seen. Each grave consists of a shaft of varying depth, but usually between six and eight feet, at the bottom of which the burial chamber opens out. Once the body and offerings had been placed inside the chamber, the entrance shaft was covered with a slab of rock, in the hope that this would disguise the presence of a tomb shaft from possible despoilers.

The cemetery continued in use long after the downfall of Carthage and well into the Roman Empire, perhaps as late as the third century A.D. Then, later still, it was abandoned and the hillside used for agricultural purposes. The existence of these tombs, however, was never forgotten and they were sacked time and again, especially during the Muslim era when passages were made from tomb to tomb. What remains of the cemetery today can only be a small part of the original burial area, and it is possible that there may be other tombs hereabouts still undiscovered. Unfortunately, in more recent years, property developers built over much of this ground before it had been properly examined by archaeologists. The Sociedad Arqueologica Ebusitana (the Archaeological Society of Ibiza) only came into being in 1903 when the great historic importance of the Puig d'es Molins and other sites on the island began to be realized. The Society carried out much useful work, as shown by the collection housed in the museum in the cathedral square, but its success attracted the attention of professional tomb robbers and a number of important objects, which should have found a home in a Spanish museum, were smuggled out of the country.

The rich archaeological finds gathered from the Puig d'es Molins has made it possible to reconstruct what these tombs were like when they were first used. Each tomb contained from one to six sarcophagi, each carved from a sandstone block and without a lid, and without ornamentation or inscription. The interior of the sarcophagi was sometimes hollow so that amphorae could be stood inside; there were also cavities for the head and feet of the corpse. As well as amphorae, a number of objects associated with the dead person would be placed with the body, including jewellery, such as rings and necklaces, earrings and scarab seals. Greek and Punic lamps, plates, jars and unguent containers made of glass, and razors for shaving have also been found and, in addition to such personal items, there were also household goods such as darning needles, weights from the family loom, mirrors and fish hooks. The objects found here date from the fifth century B.C. down to the later Roman Empire and, while predominantly of local make, also include examples of work from many peoples and places around the Mediterranean.

Many terracotta items of religious significance, especially figurines of deities, of sacred animals and masks for the dead, have been found in quantities, not only in the Puig d'es Molins, but in other sites as well, especially that of Cueva d'es Cuyram; this is a shrine, hidden away in the north-east corner of the island near San Vicente, which was dedicated, as is known from an inscription found on the spot, to Tanit. This goddess was probably originally the same as the Phoenician mother goddess Astarte, but later became identifiable with the Greek Hera. Here were found some 600 figurines together with many more heads of the same type, half buried amid ashes and the remains of burnt human bones. Sacrifice is known to have played a highly important role in Punic religion. The figurines, usually bell-shaped, seem either to represent a woman praying or Tanit herself. These can be seen in the museum in the cathedral square. Other fine examples of Tanit are to be seen in the museum on the lower slopes of the Puig d'es Molins; this small, modern building has been laid out with expert care and houses many of the finest items yet to have been unearthed in Ibiza. Not to visit the museum is to miss a most enjoyable experience.

The earliest figurines on view in Ibiza were made by the Phoenicians based on Egyptian and Assyrian styles. Later, as contacts with the Greeks developed, Phoenician craftsmen and their Punic successors followed Hellenic styles, starting with Greek–Cypriot models, continuing through the Classical Greek period down to Hellenistic and Roman times. Ibicencan products were inclined to be heavy in treatment and over-decorated. They were, moreover, largely imitative and rarely had any originality. A visit to the Greek terracotta figurines in the British Museum in London, will show the fine craftsmanship of such regional Greek centres as Rhodes, Cyrenaica and Sicily, especially when compared with the coarseness of Ibicencan work.

The Punic ceramic containers found in the tombs are also of poor quality. They were not made especially for burial, but for everyday use and, with the other articles found there, had probably been used by the dead person when alive. The earth of Ibiza, incidentally, was widely believed to have a special quality which made it highly prized. This was the capacity of neutralizing poisons of all descriptions. Pots from Ibiza in all shapes and designs must have been a valuable export commodity.

One peculiarly Punic object found in the tombs of Ibiza is the shell of the ostrich egg; a third or half the shell is cut away and the remainder decorated. Examples have been found in Sardinia and in tombs on the Spanish Peninsula as well as in Ibiza. The egg is said to have been a symbolic representation of the container in which the vital substance, needed to restore the dead to life, was kept, according to Donna Maria José Almagro Gorbea, the author of the excellent guide-book to the Puig de Molins. The designs painted on these shells came mainly from Egypt or from Asia Minor. Most of the shells which have been found date from before the fourth century B.C.; by the beginning of the first century B.C., they were apparently no longer in use.

Ibiza was undoubtedly a wealthy settlement, judging by a

reference made by Livy when describing the Second Punic War. In 217 B.C. a strong Roman force under Gnaeus Scipio made a massive raid down the east coast of Spain and then 'crossed to the island of Ebusus, where they attempted to take the chief town; it proved a laborious operation and ended after two days in failure, so when they found that they were merely wasting their time to no purpose, they turned to devastating the crops, pillaged and burned several villages and returned on board their ships with more plunder than they had taken from the mainland.' That a few pillaged villages in Ibiza could provide more wealth than a considerable stretch of the Spanish coast was indeed remarkable. It would be interesting to know whether the walls which held against Gnaeus Scipio formed the basis of those which the Muslims defended with less success in 1115 and 1235.

Throughout the Second Punic War, Ibiza remained staunchly on the side of Carthage. Even when the fortune of war was beginning to swing strongly in favour of Rome, we find Mago, the Carthaginian general, being warmly welcomed in Ibiza in 205 B.C., where, according to Livy, 'supplies were generously furnished and, in addition, weapons were given him; also men to supplement the ships' crews.'

Ibiza, unlike Carthage, was not defeated or destroyed by the Romans, but emerged with the status of an officially recognized ally of Rome. Anyway, the Ibicencans were the allies of the Romans when they invaded Majorca in 123 B.C. under the command of Quintus Cecilius Metellus, later officially dubbed 'Balearicus' to commemorate his victory over the pirate nests based on that island. Roman standards were introduced into Ibiza, including roads and water supplies. According to a Roman inscription of that period, an aqueduct to bring water to the city was financed by the Cornelius family. Gonzalez de Posada, writing in 1791, said that there were signs of an aqueduct on the road between the city and Las Salinas. Remains of Roman aqueducts were also said to have been found near Santa Eulalia and Santa Gertrudis. A fine Roman road was built from the city to Figueretas and Las Salinas, traces of which are still to be seen today on the slopes of Puig d'es Molins, close to the back of the museum. The road may in fact have separated the Punic from the Roman part of the cemetery.

Peace and prosperity on the island must have continued for most of the Roman republican period, although it was fought over, because of its strategic position, during the civil war of 81 B.C. and later, during the struggle between Julius Caesar and Pompey. Pompey was forced to fight to gain the island, which was apparently loyal to Julius Caesar, although Majorca and Minorca gave in to him without a struggle. The island seems to have suffered no long-term adversity from this involvement and may have emerged with an enhanced reputation. The Ibicencans appear to have armed themselves with the sling, as did the other islanders in the Balearics, judging by the many pellets found on the site of Puig del Valls.

As an officially recognized ally of Rome, Ibiza retained its own political identity with its own constitution, with exemption from taxes and military tribute and with the right to mint its own coins. The city's prosperity is illustrated by the great number of Ibicencan coins which have been found, not only along the length of Spain's eastern seaboard and in the other Balearic Islands, but also in Oran and Cadiz and in such inland towns as Cuenca and Lerida. Canon Macabich says that Punic traditions of energy were maintained during the Roman ascendancy. Arts and crafts must have continued in the Carthaginian style, to be modified gradually over the years, in spite of the fact that Carthage had been destroyed and that elsewhere it was usually Roman policy to extinguish all memory of a defeated enemy. Work would have continued in the mines and salt pans, in the fishing industry, in the manufacture of glass and ceramic products, and in the export of such agricultural products as dried figs. The island's population remained predominantly Punic, according to Diodorus Siculus, although there were Greek, Iberian and Roman inhabitants as well. The houses were solid and well-constructed, the city walls soundly built with fine gates. In the countryside there were vineyards and olives, but the island was only moderately fertile, so the general prosperity must largely have arisen from the industry of the population.

From Roman times until the arrival of the Muslims towards the end of the 8th century, we find little reference to Ibiza. A fresh stage in the island's history was reached in 74 A.D., when Vespasian, himself an Iberian, granted municipal rights to all cities in alliance with Rome, privileges which Ibiza had enjoyed for at least two centuries. This cannot have affected the island in any material way except perhaps for some loss of prestige.

Peace appears to have reigned until about 426 A.D. when the Vandals under Gunderic sacked the Balearics and then remained in control until early in the sixth century. They were evicted by the forces of Byzantium who successfully invaded the coast of Spain and later held the Balearics after they had been forced to relinquish their grip on the mainland. It is not known how long they remained in Ibiza after the first great Muslim naval sweep of the western Mediterranean in about 707, nor whether the troops withdrew altogether or remained as independent units under local commanders. By the middle of the ninth century, the Crescent had probably replaced the Cross throughout the Balearics.

7

South and West
The Districts of San José and San Antonio

Figueretas, a suburb of Ibiza town, begins on the far side of the Puig d'es Molins on whose slopes, which drop steeply down to the sea, white cube-shaped villas stand tightly packed amid flowering trees. At the foot of the slope, hotels and apartments border the sea along the Calle de Ramon Muntaner. The road is named after the distinguished Catalan of the fourteenth century who chronicled the exploits of the Catalan Company in which he played an active part; these adventurers, after fighting first for and afterwards against Byzantium, ended by establishing an Athenian duchy in 1313 under the Aragonese crown. Muntaner died when aged about seventy in 1336, some say in Valencia, others in Majorca, and others again here in Ibiza; the whereabouts of his grave is not known.

A pathway of steps climbs up from Figueretas over the ridge and down into the new town of Ibiza. Each step has its own oleander or pomegranite tree growing beside it, and enclosed in its own whitewashed curbstone. Local maps are not always accurate about the roads in this area. Car users cannot drive east round the Puig d'es Molins to Ibiza town but will have to go west along the Calle de Muntaner and then round into the Avenida de España, which is the main road from the town to the airport. To go in the opposite direction along the Calle only leads into a quarry whose surrounding cliffs are festooned with garbage, flung there from above.

From Figueretas southwards there are wonderful views to Corp-Mari, the 500-foot high hill at the most southerly point of the island, and of Formentera in the distance beyond. The coast here is being rapidly developed and before long is likely to be largely built up—but not entirely. Part of this coast is on the direct approach to the airport's runway, so there are restrictions against building too high to avoid danger to incoming aircraft. One hotel ignored this requirement and had subsequently to be blown up. Its debris can easily be seen from the road which leads down to Las Salinas.

There has also been some building along the road to San Jorge, where the roads from Las Salinas and the airport join, and from where there is a secondary road to the southern end of Figueretas. The houses are unpretentious, surrounded by little gardens with the inevitable geraniums. More houses will undoubtedly be erected in this area of smallholdings between the hills and the sea. Along the road and around the houses are drystone walls—a skill which has been handed down from the Islamic age, possibly from Punic times. The Ibicencan soil hereabouts is irrepressible; a few drops of rain, and the light reddish-brown earth is soon flecked with fresh green grass. Carobs, olives, almonds, whose blossom in February is the nearest thing to snow which the islanders are ever likely to see, prickly pears and great clumps of cactus, whose cumbrous great swords thrust thickly upwards—all establish themselves easily in this vigorous soil.

The dazzling whitewashed church of San Jorge (Jordi in Catalan) is one of the oldest on the island. Built either in the fourteenth or early fifteenth century, it has a severe simplicity which contrasts strongly with the florid landscape of the surrounding countryside. Its single nave with its interior Gothic arches, and the single bell in its belfry on the roof over the west entrance, are vaguely reminiscent of the primitive *Mozarab* churches in Spain, which date from the Muslim domination. Then the Christian communities, living at peace with their alien rulers, were allowed to build their own churches—but nothing is known of a *Mozarab* community in Ibiza. The two side-chapels, a larger chapel leading to the vestry and the little balcony over the west entrance indicate that the church is of a later date. A covered porch with two rows of pillars extends out from the west entrance; a market was probably held here in former days.

The most unusual feature of the church is its crenellated roof— it was also used as a fortress in which the local population took refuge when danger threatened from the corsairs. Nearly all the churches in the Ibicencan countryside were capable of being used in this way. Cannon were placed on the roof, or on a projecting strongpoint, and the marksmen took up their protected positions.

Sufficient provisions were brought up to withstand a short siege until succour could arrive from the capital, while in the courtyard, occasionally inside the church itself, there would be a well. These churches are unique in Spain, yet no two churches are exactly alike and San Jorge alone has a crenellated roof.

Extra tiers of burial chambers have recently been added to the neat little graveyard to the north side of the church. The village of San Jorge is obviously beginning to grow. On the other side of the church is the local school. Beyond, the road runs as straight as an arrow to a small group of buildings on the edge of Las Salinas. Here, all parts of the same building, is a farmhouse, a café and a small whitewashed chapel with the resonant name of San Francisco de Paula. On the west side of the chapel is the farmyard with its rabbits and hens. The exterior of the chapel and the entrance which leads both to the chapel and the farmyard are neat and well kept, but the interior of the chapel, which is obviously uncared for, is described by a local guidebook as a disaster. It seems to be rarely used.

From San Francisco the salt pans stretch south-west to the sea but are contained on the south and east sides by wooded hills. Beyond them again is the sea. There are some forty pans in which seawater is allowed to evaporate—desolate on a cloudy day and dazzling under a summer sun. A railway runs down to a little port on the southern promontory, whither ships come from far and wide to collect the salt. Mrs. Mary Stuart Boyd said that the salt was prepared to meet the differing requirements of its many customers; the Russians, for example, demanded their salt in large crystals while the Americans preferred theirs as fine as possible. During the seventeenth and eighteenth centuries, and probably earlier, slaves and criminals were the main labour force—the Ibicencans understandably preferred to look after their fields. Grasset de St. Sauveur, who was French consul in the Balearics at the beginning of the nineteenth century, said that the inhabitants, while gentle and brave, were against all innovations and had an inconceivable aversion to work; this was a characteristic noted by many later visitors, not only in Ibiza but in other parts of the Mediterranean as well, until the arrival of tourism brought opportunities for work and its rewards.

The quickest road to San Antonio Abad, the island's second

largest town, is via San Rafael, but there is a much more attractive, if longer, route via San José. On the north side are green mountains, some of which rise to 1,200 feet and more; to the south are lower hills beyond which lies the sea. One or two roads lead down to the coast at Sa Caletta and Port Roig, while Es Cubells with its hermitage, built in the nineteenth century, can be reached from San José. These secondary roads are rarely metalled but are usually passable.

San José is about nine miles from Ibiza town and is one of the larger villages on the island with a population of over 5,000. It is also the modern name of the district, originally called Las Salinas, which includes the parishes of San Jorge, San Francisco de Paula and Es Cubells. It is a scattered parish, spreading over the surrounding mountains and valleys, its whitewashed, cube-shaped, single-storey cottages or *casements* shining in the sun. The Atalaya, to the south-west of San José, is the loftiest point on the island, over 1,500 feet high, and from the top there are wonderful views as far as the Peninsula as well as to Formentera. The church of San José, painted in dazzling white, was built in the eighteenth century; its belfry stands over the centre of its west façade above the entrance. It has the usual single nave, together with four chapels on each side and a gallery running above them. There is also a gallery at the west end over the entrance, supported by the wide, shallow arch which is found in the Baroque churches of Majorca. There is a rather ornate altar on which stands a St. Joseph from a much earlier period, perhaps dating from when the church was first built. The interior is unremarkable but light and airy. Outside the walls of the forecourt support a corrugated roof. At the side of the church is the priest's house. On the far side of the road are several souvenir shops.

A little beyond San José the main road swings north, and secondary roads lead off, not only to Es Cubells, but to Cala Vadella and Cala Moli, both centres of new holiday home developments. Groups of new houses are also to be found further up the coast at Cala Codola and at Port del Torrent on the approaches to San Antonio. There is considerable uniformity in the way that many of these developments are laid out, but trees and flowering shrubs will in due course soften the impact and there are always wonderful views, especially towards the south-west where the Isla Vedra and its satellite, La Vedranell, tower steeply out of the sea. The Vedra, its bare rock sparsely covered with scrub, is inhabited by wild goats.

There is a distant view of the sea for most of the five miles along the road between San José and San Antonio. Almost halfway, a road winds uphill to the pleasant village of San Augustin and its simple whitewashed church with its square façade at the west end, its round-arched entrance with tiny circular window above, surmounted on top by a belfry housing a single bell. From here the views extend over a large part of the district, originally known as Portumany, with the Isla Conejera in the far west guarding the entrance to the great sweeping bay of San Antonio, around much of which San Antonio Abad, with its hotels and apartments, has now spread. San Augustin is said to produce some of the best wine on the island, but only in sufficient quantities for local consumption.

William de Montgri and his associates found in 1235 that the island was divided for administrative purposes into five districts—Alhauech, Xarch, Benizamid, Portumany and Algarb. They had already agreed before the expedition set sail that each should receive territory in proportion to the number of men and munitions that he supplied. As the Portuguese Infante and the Count of Roussillon each brought the same number of men with them, and as de Montgri's troops were equal to both these groups, it was agreed after the victory that de Montgri should receive half the island and that the other two be given a quarter each. The Archbishop-elect of Tarragona took over Algarb (Las Salinas) and Benizamid (Balanzat or the northern part of the island), Don Pedro received Xarch (Santa Eulalia) and Nuno Sanchez Portumany (San Antonio); the fifth district, Alhauech, was divided equitably between them. Of these five names, all are of Arabic origin with the exception of Portumany which is a corruption of Portus Magnus, the name the Romans gave to San Antonio. Today, the district of San Antonio includes the parishes of San Rafael, Santa Ines and San Mateo.

When seen from a distance, San Antonio gives the impression of a modern, gleaming city of glass and concrete, spread round the great bay with its fine, sandy, pine-shaded beaches. Arrive at its centre, however, and it reveals itself as a small village, around which tourism has planted a variety of buildings—some good, some not so good. There is no depth to the town. Move more than 300 yards inland from the beach, and you are likely to find yourself in open country. The resort is packed in summer with visitors from all parts of western and northern Europe but is empty in winter.

The only building in San Antonio of any age or of any historic interest is the church, whose patron saint has given the town his name. It was built in the fourteenth century and is second in seniority only to the church of St. Mary in Ibiza town which, before 1782, was the only parish church for the island and for neighbouring Formentera. Chapels were erected in the country districts, or *cuartons*, as early as the fourteenth century, but chaplains resided at them only during Lent; for the rest of the year they were expected to dwell in Ibiza town and assist in the work of St. Mary's. There must have been occasions when the chaplains were absent from their districts even during Lent, because of the corsair raids. For example, records show that as early as 1383 Saracens landed here at San Antonio, set fire to the houses and took away nineteen inhabitants as captives. By the middle of the seventeenth century, however, the ecclesiastical authorities decided that with the decline in the number and strength of these raids from North Africa, and with the increase in the local population, chaplains should take up permanent residence at the outlying chapels. This may have been when the church that we see here today first took shape. Then in 1782, when the church of St. Mary was made a cathedral, the chapels became parish churches.

The church of San Antonio stands confined in a not unattractive little square. Commercial buildings have been added on to its north wall. The church is situated a little way back from the resort's fine, open quay and on a slight rise, so that the cannon, at one time sited on the fortified tower at the east end of the church, could cover the entire area then occupied by the little fishing village. Its main entrance is from the south side through the round arches of the surrounding wall and into a cobbled courtyard which is only partly covered. On the roof, over this entrance, is an unusual two-arched belfry. All is gleaming white except for the defence tower on the east side which is of unadorned, solid sandstone. Inside there is the usual single nave with four chapels on each side, one of which on the south side has been adapted to serve as the main entrance from the courtyard. There is another entrance at the west end under a wide, shallow arch in the Majorcan style of Baroque, supporting a balcony. The ceiling is ogival and could conceivably be eighteenth rather than fourteenth-century work. Except for its shape, the church is typically Ibicencan, including the well, which was recently rediscovered under the floor of the nave.

The quay runs along the north side of the town, close to where the road from San José joins that from San Rafael. Fishing boats once moored here but they have now been largely replaced in summer by excursion boats which leave for the largely unspoilt coasts to the north and west. Northwards, at least, there is no road along the coast and the rough track which runs inland to Santa Ines is only suitable for farm carts. Santa Ines itself stands amid farms in one of the most attractive areas of the island, but when driving there it is best to go via San Rafael, only five miles away from San Antonio.

The road to San Rafael is straight, uphill and perhaps of Roman origin. The little village is more concentrated than is usual round the road junction at its centre. From here a good modern highway stretches away to join up with the main road to the north of the island and with that which links the capital with Santa Eulalia. In winter and spring, the village must be conscious of its exposed position because of the fierce west winds which assail it. For this reason, the church of San Rafael stands just over the brow of the hill to the east and its courtyard has a protective wall on its west side. For the same reason, many peasant cottages in this area have no windows facing west. The church itself is long, buttressed like the cathedral, and gleaming white.

The distance from San Rafael to Santa Ines is about seven miles. The road runs through glorious, rustic country with earth the colour of paprika. In addition to the carob, olive and almond trees which grow in the gardens and fields, there are many fig trees so elderly and wind-battered that their branches, which still give a plentiful supply of fruit, have to be supported on staves.

The little white church of Santa Ines stands on the edge of a wide open space, which marks the centre of the village; it serves not only the three country cottages standing close by in their flourishing gardens, but the whole of the surrounding area, where there are many farms. Some churches, as we know, were built on the sites of mosques, but not these country churches. The most brazen-voiced muezzin could not call to prayer a fraction of his congregation from the church of Santa Ines, especially when the west wind was blowing.

To the north and west of the village there are pleasant walks with remarkable views, especially over the rugged cliffs to the sea beyond. Pine woods fringe the edge of the cliffs and there are no sandy beaches below. It is highly unlikely that this wild, magnificent coastline will be spoiled for many years. The older farmhouses in the area are not whitewashed and the natural colouring of the walls blends well with the countryside.

On the coast between San Antonio and Santa Ines there are no villages or hotels north of Cala Grasio with its little wooded inlets. From Santa Ines to San Mateo by a very rough country road is only three miles distance through the most rustic part of the island, dominated by the Camp Vei, north of Santa Ines, which rises to over 1,200 feet. Motorists may feel safer if they take the excellent road back to San Rafael, travel across to the San Miguel road and up as far as Santa Gertrudis, before turning on to the good secondary road to San Mateo, the whole distance being about seventeen miles. San Mateo is said to produce wine equal to that of San Augustin; grapes from here were once exported to Majorca. The small whitewashed church, built at the end of the eighteenth century, has no outstanding features but is delightfully situated beneath a pine-covered hill at the end of an empty road which has wandered through terraced fields and woods. It is in such inland villages as Santa Ines and San Mateo that a few of Ibiza's ancient traditions may still linger on.

8

North and East
The Districts of San Juan Bautista and Santa Eulalia

Some commercial building—warehouses and garages—has developed recently along the first 200 or 300 yards of the Ibiza–San Rafael road, and along the road which follows the harbour front to run north to Portinatx, San Juan Bautista, San Miguel, Cala San Vicente and Santa Eulalia. The second of these two roads quickly begins to run alongside the well-watered Pla (plain) de Vila with its *norias* or waterwheels introduced by the Arabs, and its *feixes* or oblong plots of market garden, surrounded by irrigation canals and entered through tall, whitewashed gateways over little bridges. The island, in spite of its usually dry summers, has always had immense, easily-tapped water reserves—at least until recently—because of the large deposits of clay between the limestone beds, which prevent the rainfall from draining away. Ibiza is the only Balearic island to possess a river, that of Santa Eulalia, which reaches the sea just to the south of the town of that name. So abundant were these supplies thought to have been that there has been talk of water being piped across the sea to Formentera for the tourist hotels planned there.

In February, 1973, however, the Spanish government ordered a halt to the construction of all further hotels, apartments and villas on Ibiza because official estimates revealed that the island's freshwater supply may be inadequate by 1980. In the meanwhile a hydrographic survey was commissioned to find out whether there are any new sources of water which can be tapped. A danger signal, which alerted the authorities to the situation, was the fact that wells drilled along the coast were proving to be increasingly salty. This indicated that the freshwater supplies beneath the soil were being used up more quickly than they could be replenished by the winter rains and might be in danger of contamination through seawater seeping into them.

About four miles out of Ibiza, the road divides into two. The more westerly leads to San Miguel and its port, thirteen miles from Ibiza, while the other ends at Portinatx, seventeen miles away; a branch of the latter goes east to Cala San Vicente via San Juan Bautista. The roads are well surfaced, wide enough for two vehicles to pass in comfort and virtually empty of traffic for most months of the year.

The only village, little more than a hamlet, of any significance on the way to San Miguel is that of Santa Gertrudis, which is just off the main road towards San Mateo. There is a short, wide, tree-lined village street to the west of the whitewashed parish church, whose single-arched belfry stands off-centre above the west façade. Inside, the usual single nave under a barrel-vaulted roof has two chapels on each side. The chapel on the north side nearest the altar extends into a north transept, in which seats face south towards the altar. On each side of the chapels square-shaped pillars crowned with curious rustic capitals support the ceiling.

The church of San Miguel, first erected in the fourteenth century but with eighteenth-century additions, stands high on a hill above the highway which continues through the tiny modern hamlet below to the Puerto de San Miguel some two miles further on. It is reached by a steeply climbing street which passes comfortable village houses ending in front of a whitewashed wall. The stone-flagged courtyard beyond is reached through three rounded arch-ways in the wall, and is flanked by two rows of whitewashed cottages—one on each side. Immediately in front of the doorway into the church a wooden-roofed portico is supported on whitewashed pillars. Once inside, it becomes clear that the entrance leads from the south side into the middle of the church with the altar on the right. The single nave building is in the shape of the letter T, with a north and south transept, the latter partly decorated with a colour stencil design. There is a gallery at the west end.

The priest's accommodation is over the church and the bell-rope which falls from the little belfry, situated on the parapet of the roof, is conveniently within reach of his first-floor balcony. His upstairs dwelling rooms and the various storage lofts make the overall church structure look very much bigger than the space occupied by the place of worship. Other churches on the island are similarly built, including Santa Gertrudis. A walk round to the back of the church will reveal how solidly it is made of sandstone, here without any adornment or whitewash, giving the impression that it is as much fortress as church. Several new villas stand close by.

The road to the Puerto de San Miguel twists and turns downhill through pineclad slopes to the little bay on the north-west coast, whose mediaeval name was Balanzat, the name both of one of the four *cuartons* into which the island was divided by its conquerors in 1235, and of one of Ibiza's oldest families. On both sides of the inlet the hills rise steeply. Sheltering under the eastern flank, which is the higher, stand two vast west-facing hotels, the colour of granite. A road climbs up the slopes behind the hotels through pinewoods where holiday villas may soon prank, looking down onto one of the grandest, wildest bays of Ibiza.

Out beyond the bay rises the Isla de Murada, where the remains of a Roman wall are said to stand. On the cliffs to the west is the Torre del Mula, from the top of which the approach of raiders would have been signalled to San Miguel, just visible on its inland hill. These towers, sometimes known as *atalayas* or watch-towers, were built at intervals round the coast, as in Majorca and Minorca, mainly during the sixteenth century. A number were furnished with artillery, usually one or two cannon, depending upon the site and perhaps upon their availability; the churches capable of being defended were included in this system. Each tower had two or more guards. There was also a local militia, inaugurated at the time of the Reconquest, which could be sent to any part of the island needing help. The alarm would be given by bonfires, whose flames would be visible by night and its smoke by day, and by the ringing of bells. This coastal defence system was finally disbanded as recently as 1867.

From San Miguel a rough road travels across country for some five miles to join the Portinatx highway, just south of the branch which turns off to San Juan Bautista. The more cautious will probably prefer to drive back to Santa Gertrudis, turn left on meeting the road from San Rafael and then left again along the road from Ibiza to the far north. The highway rises gently nearly all the way. On the left is the little village of San Lorenzo with its white, unpretentious eighteenth-century church. Close by is the hamlet of Balafi with its white houses standing on a ridge and its two reddish round towers. Here the inhabitants would seek shelter when danger threatened from the corsairs by climbing up rope ladders which they would draw up after them.

After leaving behind the branch road to San Juan Bautista, the highway rises sharply to cross the ridge of the northern mountain chain and then descends by many hairpin bends to reach the northern shore. The scenery is magnificent. The sea comes crashing into the limestone cliffs, which vary considerably in height, and has carved little coves out of the rocks, in some of which sand has collected. First there is the Cala Charraca, then the Cala Chucia, then the Cala Portinatx, with its sheltered, sandy bay. Here, until a year or two ago, there were only two small pensions. Now three enormous hotels, two of them close together, have been built overlooking the sea and a fourth is planned. Villas are beginning to be built among the pine-covered slopes round the bay. The firm sandy beach is clean.

Between Portinatx and Cala San Vicente, the wild rugged coast is completely empty of human habitation and the hinterland without tracks or roadways. The only way to reach Cala San Vicente is to take the road leading back over the mountainous ridge and through San Juan Bautista, which is a village of little interest. There is a white eighteenth-century church, which has since undergone alteration, and a small town hall in the village square. San Juan is the senior parish in the north of the island. The road onwards to Cala San Vicente becomes increasingly attractive, especially when the great rugged hills, which protect the small resort, come into view. Between San Juan and the Cala lies the village of San Vicente. Its little white church on a hill, the most recent of Ibiza's country churches, was built some 140 years ago, and the village boasts a cinema.

The Cala San Vicente faces south-east towards the enchanting islet of Tagomago. Until about 1965 this bay was deserted, the haunt of seabirds and the occasional picnic party. Then towards the end of the sixties, a large hotel was erected on the narrow platform of shore between the Punta Grosa, which rises steeply behind, and the sea. Three further hotels have since been squeezed into the available space. What has been built here is out of scale with the surrounding landscape, although their size would arouse no comment if added to the hotels around the bay of San Antonio.

Behind the hotels, a rough road mounts steeply up the Punta Grosa, at the far end of which there is a lighthouse; along the route there are wonderful views of sea and sky, of Tagomago and of the heights above San Carlos. A shrine of the Punic goddess Tanit is tucked away in the rugged country beyond.

Although rarely marked on tourist maps, a track of the very roughest sort runs south from Cala San Vicente to San Carlos. It hugs the wooded hillside, overlooking the sea, where one or two secluded white villas have recently been built, and then crosses rough open country, mainly farmland, to join up with the good road from San Carlos to the coast. This track is at present made of earth and its potholes become great pools of muddy water after a downpour, but it could easily be converted into a metalled road which would inevitably bring hotels and villas to one of the least-spoiled corners of the island. The process of opening up this side of the island has already started, not only at Cala San Vicente but at the Playa d'es Figueral which lies at the end of a good road from San Carlos. Already one or two hotels and blocks of apartment flats have been erected here where three years ago there was only a little beach bar.

Looking at these golden sun-filled landscapes, at the green wooded hills, at the open valleys and grass-covered plains of pale-red earth, at the almond, carob, fig and olive trees and, here and there, the traditional, white cube-shaped cottages, all this bounded by the blue of the sky and the deeper blue of the sea, it is easy to understand how a lyrical school of poets has developed in Ibiza and achieved a wide recognition in Spain. The most senior among them was Canon Isidor Macabich, the island's historian who died in 1973; perhaps the most distinguished living members of this school are Mariano Villangomez and Francisco José Mayans. These poets have celebrated an Ibiza which is beginning to fade, the island which existed before the large-scale introduction of tourism. Those of our grandchildren who may be interested in exploring what life was like on a remote Mediterranean island before the advent of radio, television, airports and economy tours will find an answer in the work of these poets. Few islands can be as fortunate as Ibiza in its interpreters.

San Carlos is another scattered community with an attractive church surrounded by a few cottages amid low hills and trees. The

brilliantly white church was built in the eighteenth century and
has a double sloping roof, a single-arched belfry on one side and
a covered forecourt in front of the west entrance. Inside, the single
nave has a barrel-vaulted ceiling, picked out in pale washes, and
there is a fine modern altar, not altogether dissimilar to a Minorcan
taula in design, made from rough hewn stone. Built on to the
south side of the church is the two storied house of the priest,
covered with bougainvillaea, which gives the building as a whole a
rustic simplicity. Nearby, along the road to Santa Eulalia, were
Ibiza's lead mines, now abandoned, which were worked from very
early days in the history of the island; their site can be clearly seen.

Further south again, the east coast of the island is now under-
going development, especially at Es Cana and S'Argamasa. Until
a few years ago, Es Cana was a simple village huddled round its
harbour. Now great hotel and apartment complexes stand on the
red soil of the area, backed by pinewoods. The village is reached
along a pleasant rural road from Santa Eulalia, which runs through
fields and woods with only an occasional white or unstuccoed
cottage among them. There are no large country houses in Ibiza,
as there are in Majorca, because at the Reconquest the land was
split up only into smallholdings by the three leaders to avoid the
creation of powerful land magnates. S'Argamasa is reached off the
same road. Here, on the sheltered side of the island, the climate can
be warm and inviting in the opening weeks of the year; there is a
marvellous contrast between the red earth and the fresh green of
spring grass, seen in the luminous brilliance of a sunny February
morning, unmisted by summer's heat.

Santa Eulalia is the third largest settlement on the island. The
oldest part stands on the hill, whose summit is crowned by the
church, just to the north of the river, the only one in the Balearic
group of islands. From the hill, the town is spreading rapidly north-
eastwards, parallel to the sea, with the usual hotels, apartments,
shops and villas. Although these developments are taking place
largely on the grid system, flowering trees and open spaces between
them give Santa Eulalia a pleasant air. The saint which the town's
name celebrates was a popular Catalan figure. St. Eulalia of
Mérida, who was also of Barcelona, was only twelve years old
when the Edicts of Diocletian were issued, compelling all citizens
to pay homage to the gods of the Empire. Her mother, conscious

that Eulalia desired martyrdom, fled with her from Catalonia in about 304 to distant Mérida in Estremadura; there, however, the girl found an opportunity of insulting the divinities. The Imperial judge did everything possible to persuade one so young to recant but, on her repeated refusal, he was eventually forced by law to order her execution. This was described in a hymn written at the end of the fourth century by Prudentius who speaks of white doves flying out of her mouth as she was burnt to death and of how the whole forum where the sentence took place was covered with snow. Her feast is celebrated on 12th February.

The most fascinating building in Santa Eulalia is, as usual, the church, which is reached after a steep climb up the hill past typical white Ibicencan cottages. A deep, cool, stone-flagged forecourt with low-built arches to keep out the sun stands in front of, but apart from, the west entrance of the church. Markets would probably have been held here before the village spread beyond the hill, and its well still serves the neighbouring cottages. The church itself was built during the sixteenth century and has something of the character of a fortification, both because of its severity of line and because the unadorned, semi-circular bastion that protrudes from the east end of the church is said to be half of an ancient round *atalaya* which stood here before the church was erected. The building is whitewashed inside as well as out; the single nave has a barrel-vaulted ceiling and, apart from the great Baroque wooden altar, is completely plain. On the south side is a large chapel over which rises a tiled dome with a pretty lantern at its apex. On the north side is the cheerful little cemetery, reached by the path past the priest's modern house and the once fortified apse.

The priest's new house and the excellent condition of the church is perhaps explained by what happened here during the Spanish Civil War of 1936–39. When the conflagration started towards the end of July 1936, Minorca declared itself for the Republican government of the day, but Majorca and Ibiza were held on behalf of General Franco and the Nationalist movement. Elliot Paul, an American writer who was then living in Santa Eulalia, described events during the weeks which immediately followed the start of the Civil War in his book, *Life and Death of a Spanish Town*. Early in August, a Republican task force, convoyed by a light cruiser, two destroyers and four submarines, was sent to the Balearics to seize Majorca and Ibiza for the Republic. After taking Formentera, this force approached Ibiza and landed 4,000 militiamen from the mainland close to Santa Eulalia. Elliot Paul, whose sympathies lay with the Republic, admits that the church of Santa Eulalia was set on fire by these troops and that similar action was taken against churches elsewhere on the island; the reason given for this was that arms were found in them intended for enemies of the Republic. The churches of the neighbouring villages of Jesus, San Miguel and San Jorge were however spared. Soon after the burning of the church of Santa Eulalia, the Republican task force, under the impression that Ibiza was fully secured, departed for Majorca.

Ibiza might have remained with the Republicans if they had been successful in Majorca instead of allowing themselves to be repelled by the Nationalists. Shortly afterwards, Ibiza was occupied by Italian troops, at which point Elliot Paul, his family and other expatriates living in Ibiza departed. At one stage during the Civil War, the Republican government denounced Italy for her supposed intention of incorporating the Balearic Islands into Mussolini's Italian Empire.

Fishing is still an active industry of the island and Santa Eulalia is one of its centres. Elliot Paul wrote, 'I think there are no better fishing grounds than those lying north and east of Ibiza, and let no one imagine that the tales of hardship and death and perpetual danger apply to the happy-go-lucky crews who set out from Santa Eulalia. There is no ice in the rigging, no bullying skipper, no waiting women wringing their hands on the shore. On the contrary, if the weather was a least bit rough they stayed in town, strolling from café to café and by nightfall would be roaring but never belligerent. There was no reason for them to risk their necks. For thousands of years, the sea which lay within convenient rowing distance, had yielded richly whenever the waters were calm, and if the people who remained on land, either in Ibiza or Valencia or Barcelona, could not have fish on a certain day, they could eat lamb or goat, and, in winter, pork or *sobrasada* [a delicious spiced sausage].' Paul made a further point about the fishermen. The harvest of the sea is not achieved in the same way as sheaves of wheat or tubs of grapes. 'If a fisherman had to plant a *mero* [a type of Mediterranean bass], bend over in the hot sun for months at a stretch in order to pluck it, then thresh it and gather it into barns, no fish would be available for mankind.'

Once over the bridge across the river of Santa Eulalia, there are two ways back to Ibiza town—a fast road which joins up with that from Portinatx and a second, more picturesque but rather slower route via Cala Llonga, Ca'n Furnet and Jesus. To take the latter route involves a sharp left turn, once over the bridge. Between this road and the sea are a number of residential developments on the slopes of the hills which face across the river to Santa Eulalia. Cala Llonga is some three miles farther on. It must have been one of the prettiest bays on the east coast. Now it is fully developed as a resort.

Between Cala Llonga and Jesus the road runs through peaceful, rolling country with spreading pinewoods which shelter a new golf course. Further inland, the red earth of the fields is terraced to make full use of all available soil. Ca'n Furnet is a typical if unremarkable village, and so is Jesus, except for the church of Our Lady of Jesus and the remarkable painting it contains. The church stands down a lane just to the south of the Ibiza–Cala Llonga road, and consists of what was probably at one time a conventual building, the church itself and the priest's house, terraced together in that order. The entrance to the church is a simple doorway under a round arch with three little windows in the white wall above, surmounted by a typical single-arched belfry. The church is not always open outside the times of service, nor are visitors automatically encouraged because they rarely come to worship and often depart without placing a coin in the offertory. It is a good idea to enquire about the priest's movements, if he happens to be away, at the little bar at the beginning of the lane. If he is due back shortly, it is worth waiting and in the meanwhile sampling the bar's homemade *frigola*, an Ibicencan liqueur, made in many homes, which tastes something like the Pyrenean *Izarra*.

The church was built in the sixteenth century as part, first of a Franciscan and afterwards of a Dominican monastery; and this may account for so fine a picture in what is now a small country church. Certainly, the first impression, on stepping into the nave from the west entrance, of this great altarpiece, which stretches up to the ceiling, is breathtaking. It is by Rodrigo de Osona the younger whose *Epiphany* can be seen in the National Gallery,

London. He and his father, of the same name, worked in Valencia in the latter part of the fifteenth and the early part of the sixteenth century. Chandler R. Post writes that they were the first local artists to work in what can be called even an approximation to the style of the Italian Renaissance, which made itself felt earlier in Valencia than elsewhere in Spain. There had been close and continuing contact between Italy and the east coast of Spain from 1443 onwards as a result of the acquisition of the Kingdom of Naples in that year by Alfonso V of Aragon.

The central panel portrays the Virgin and Child enthroned under a canopy which is held up by six angels. Four more angels play musical instruments below the throne. Many of the apostles are portrayed on the panels, which surround the centrepiece, and on the *guardapolva*, the frame which protects the sides and top of the composition. On the predella below there are seven scenes concerned with the Madonna's association with the Redemption; the middle scene shows a marvellous Spanish Christ. There are echoes of Botticelli and his pagan charm in the central panel of the work and something, according to Post, of the older Osona's restraint and of Mantegna in the predella. This is perhaps the greatest work of art in the Balearic Islands.

9

Formentera

From the ramparts behind Ibiza cathedral, from the top of the
Puig d'es Molins, from the hotel terraces of Figueretas and from
wherever there is a view of the Mediterranean to the south, the
island of Formentera can be seen stretching across the horizon.
Sometimes, it appears as if there are two islands for the heights
at its eastern and western ends are separated by a plain which barely
rises above sea level and in certain lights seems to merge with the
sea itself. In between Formentera and Ibiza there is a scattering of
islets, the largest of which are the Isla Espalmador, the Isla Espardell and the Isla de Ahorcados; the others are little more than
rocks. The Isla Espalmador and the Isla de Ahorcados stand
directly in line between the Punta de Portas, Ibiza's most southerly
point, and Trocadors, the most northerly tip of Formentera,
marking the route taken by the boat service connecting the two
islands.

It is in the nature of islands to encourage and entice visitors, and
Formentera is no exception. There are regular services from the
quay at Ibiza starting close to the obelisk which commemorates
the island's privateers. The journey can however be extremely
rough on occasion, especially when crossing the stretch of open
water known as Los Freos, or the Narrows, between southernmost
Ibiza and La Sabina, Formentera's harbour. The winds here seem
to come from all directions at once when the sea is particularly
rough. But do not be discouraged by this possibility as Gaston
Vuillier was when he asked the Canon of Ibiza's advice about
visiting the smaller island. 'The priest strongly dissuaded me from
making the attempt. "It is an arid rock containing two bitter lakes
and three fortified churches, like those you will see in the environs
of Ibiza. For the sake of these, it is not worthwhile being detained

on the island for several weeks in dullness and misery. The wind is favourable now, but if it should change while you are there, it would be impossible for you to return." I owned the wisdom of his advice and reluctantly abandoned my plan of visiting the lonely islet.'

The distance between Ibiza harbour and La Sabina is eleven miles and the journey takes an hour to an hour and a half, depending upon the boat and the state of the weather. The regular morning and afternoon services are not easily dissuaded these days from making the crossing, but the trips specially designed for tourists are more circumspect, out of consideration for their passengers, and may not set out if the day promises to be bad. The journey can therefore be regarded as a challenge which should be accepted for the exhilaration of being on the open sea, even for so short a time, for the charm of Formentera itself—and it is probable that Vuillier's Canon never visited the island—and for the new perspective one gets of Ibiza from a distance. It is however advisable, if the sea is at all choppy, to make sure before leaving Ibiza that the boat will definitely be coming back the same day and to check once more with the skipper on reaching La Sabina the time he will be returning.

On leaving Ibiza harbour the boat sails either close to the shore or a little further out, depending on the weather. There is a fine view of the Dalt Vila and the Puig d'es Molins to the west and of the Isla Grosa with its lighthouse to the east. As the boat proceeds southward you can clearly see the ruins of the hotel which was blown up to prevent it endangering aircraft approaching the island's airport; then comes the Torre de Sal Rossa, one of the watch-towers of the island's defence system, guarding the approaches to the salt pans at Las Salinas; the caves in the steep limestone cliffs of Corp-Mari; and finally the little tower at the end of Punta de Portas. If a strong wind is blowing from the north-west, the direction from which usually to expect rough weather, it is only now, as the boat moves away from the shelter of the land, that the passengers become conscious of the sea's movement.

On a bad day, a keen eye, knowing where to look, will detect the spray of waves beating against the islets and rocks in Los Freos. To pass through these narrows in rough weather is to know the feelings, if any, of an ice cube in a vigorously handled cocktail shaker. On such days, it is difficult to see in passing much of the

smaller Isla de Ahorcados or of the much larger Isla Espalmador
because of the spray and spume of the waves crashing against them.
The Isla de Ahorcados—the island of the hanged men—appears
to be bare of everything except the toughest of rock plants. Here
those condemned to death in Ibiza were once brought for execution
so that the larger island should not be defiled by their killing. At
its southern end is a lighthouse. There is also a lighthouse at the
northern tip of the Isla Espalmador; between them is the main
shipping lane for vessels sailing between Ibiza and Formentera
en route for some distant destination. Espalmador, whose name
refers to the caulking of ships, is likely to be declared a nature
reserve for birds and fish. The islet is partly cultivated and has an
ancient defence tower.

The remainder of the crossing passes to the west of the long,
narrow spit of sand dunes which form the most northerly point of
Formentera; here grow dwarf pine and tamarind trees and the area
is very popular with sun-bathers. The well-enclosed harbour of
La Sabina is not particularly attractive; apart from the boats on the
ferry service to Ibiza, only a few fishing boats berth here and, of
course, yachts in summer. Around the harbour are scattered a few
buildings housing local travel agencies and car hire firms. Taxis
are also available and there is an occasional bus service.

Formentera has a population of under 4,000, covers 38 square
miles, and consists of one administrative district, which is divided
into three parishes. The capital is San Francisco Javier, about a
mile and a half inland from La Sabina. Economically the island is
looking increasingly towards tourism as a source of income, but
fishing and the production of salt still play a significant role. The
salt pans are situated at the beginning of the northern sand dunes;
to their south-west is the great Estany Pudent, a wide stretch of
malodorous water as the name Pudent ('stinking') implies. The
hotels here are as yet few and scattered, but a large one has recently
been built on the southern side of the island and more will no doubt
spring up if and when the piping of water from Ibiza becomes
practical. Doubts about the adequacy of the longterm supply to
meet the growing demands from hotels and villas on both islands
must first be smoothed away.

Named Ofiusa by the Greeks, the island was called Frumentaria
by the Romans, signifying an abundance of wheat; the modern

name is a corruption of this since *forment* is the Catalan word for wheat. Much of the land is under cultivation but the soil on the rocky ground is sometimes thin and wherever there is a change of level, however slight, walls about eighteen inches high have been built to contain it. In many places around San Francisco and San Fernando the underlying rock emerges.

San Francisco is really only a village but stands at the junction of the island's roads—roads going to Cala Sahona and Cabo Berberia in the south-west and south, to Playa d'es Pujols (perhaps the most developed of the new tourist resorts) in the north, to Playa de Mitjorn which runs along much of the southern shore, and to the far eastern end of the island, past San Fernando and Es Calo, to the Faro (lighthouse) de Formentera, high up on the edge of the cliffs from where, on a clear day, it is sometimes just possible to see Majorca. At the centre of the village is the little fortified church, whitewashed like those in Ibiza. At one side it is joined to an ugly dwelling house which is never shown in photographs. The church, which is quite small inside, has an unusual painting looking like a hanging carpet at the east end behind the altar. The west facade is completely without decoration and the large stone blocks of which it is constructed can be seen under the thinning whitewash. Cannon were once mounted on the roof.

The church was started in 1719 and dedicated seven years later. It was the first to be built on Formentera in recent centuries. Before the beginning of the eighteenth century Formentera had been virtually uninhabited, for so small and open an island is impossible to defend. Nothing is known of its earliest inhabitants who may have been Phoenicians or Carthaginians, attracted here by the fishing and salt pans. Vikings are said to have seized the island in 859, but this was probably for a short time only. We have already seen from Canon Macabich's research into the records kept in Ibiza that Formentera was in constant use as a haven for pirates after the Reconquest. In Colin Campbell's *The Ancient and Modern History of the Balearic Islands*, based on the work of the Majorcan historians, Dameto and Mut, and published at the beginning of the eighteenth century, there is a brief reference to conditions there after the abandonment of the island by its inhabitants: 'There are a kind of wild asses, which as they exceed others in Figure and Stature, so they are more unserviceable; they go in Droves, and are not to be tamed by Industry or Skill.' Wild pigs, reverting to nature from farm-bred stock, were the other denizens of the island. Campbell also reported that the island was once rich with corn, 'as to be seen by the Ruins of more than 1,000 Granaries', that in ancient times it was well populated and had its own bishop. These claims have not been supported by more recent historians.

In 1453, Alfonso V of Aragon, having been told of Formentera's desolation and its use as a shelter by corsairs, granted the island in fief to one Juan Marti. In return, Marti promised the King to build a fortified tower, which would encourage people to return and settle on the island; the tower was to be started within one year of the agreement and completed within five. Salt from the island's pans was not to be sold for personal profit but through the usual channels as laid down by the municipality of Ibiza. The local authorities, however, disapproved of the whole arrangement, so Marti's plan was never implemented.

Throughout the sixteenth century, Formentera continued to be used constantly by North African and Turkish raiders, especially the long sandy beach of the Playa de Mitjorn in the south, up which galleots could be pulled for safety when the *tramontana* or north wind blew. The galleot, as distinct from the very much larger and more cumbrous galley, was the favourite warship of the Turks. It could be manoeuvred with the ease of a modern destroyer as compared with the galley, which might be likened to a battleship. A further advantage enjoyed by a galleot was that its oarsmen were all freemen, consisting of Turks and other Muslims who became part of the fighting force in battle. Galleys, on the other hand, needed many more oarsmen, who were almost invariably slaves and had to be guarded during action. The main advantages of the galley were its greater speed and its ability to carry far heavier loads.

In 1529 an important victory was gained by the Turks over a Spanish squadron off the Playa de Mitjorn. Kheir-ed-Din Barbarossa, who later became the High Admiral of the Ottoman navy, had ordered a large raiding party consisting of fourteen galleots under the command of Aydin Rais to ransack the Balearic Islands. In doing this he was taking advantage of the absence of most of the Spanish fleet from its home waters to conduct Charles V to Italy for his coronation as Holy Roman Emperor. The Muslim raiders, after plundering the Balearics, made a sweep through the Bay of

Valencia, where they captured many ships and slaves. They also took on board a number of *Morisco* families, vassals of the Conde de Oliva, an important nobleman of Valencia, who wished to be transported to Islamic territory where they could practice their religion in freedom. The *Moriscos* were Muslims who, in the earlier days of the Reconquest, had been allowed to live and worship in their own communities under Christian rule, very much as the *Mozarabs*, members of Christian communities, had been tolerated in Al-Andalus during the reign of the Cordovan caliphate. For to Muslims, both Christians and Jews were 'people of the book', people with advanced and sophisticated religions from which Islam itself had drawn part of its beliefs. By the sixteenth century however, intolerance and persecution were to the forefront both among Christians and Muslims and Aydin Rais was pleased not only to help his co-religionists escape to freedom but also to relieve the Conde de Oliva of much treasure. Having done so, he immediately made for Formentera in order to water his ships and perhaps redistribute his load.

The Conde de Oliva, furious at his loss, at once made contact with General Portundo, commanding eight large Spanish galleys which had escorted Charles V to Genoa, told him of the situation and reported that the Muslim raiding party had been seen making for Formentera. De Oliva promised Portundo 10,000 ducats if both the *Morisco* slaves and his treasure were returned intact to him. Portundo agreed to give chase to the corsairs, even though he had no troops on board. The leading four galleys caught Aydin by surprise, but Portundo, instead of pressing home the attack, decided to wait for the remaining galleys to catch up. He was also faced with the problem of seizing the treasure, which meant that he dare not fire on the galleots for fear of sinking them. Aydin, mistaking caution for cowardice, grabbed the initiative and, manoeuvring his fourteen galleots into position, made a furious attack upon the Spaniards, which was entirely successful. General Portundo was mortally wounded in the fight upon his flagship and seven out of eight of his galleys were towed triumphantly into Algiers. The only Spanish galley which escaped managed to reach the nearest Ibicencan shelter, which was the port of Las Salinas.

By the end of the seventeenth century the tide had turned in

favour of Christendom in the Balearics and we find the first tenta-
tive steps to repopulate the island taking place in 1697, when
parcels of land were given to anyone prepared to settle there. The
building of the church of San Francisco Javier only a few years
later showed that the resettlement policy was proving successful.

The establishment of a reliable lighthouse system must have
come somewhat later. Vicente Blasco Ibanez, the novelist, wrote
earlier this century that, until this happened, the inhabitants of
Formentera would on dark nights light fires, especially on the
islets which lay between them and Ibiza, to entice ships at sea to
wreck themselves on their beaches. Once this had been achieved,
the shipwrecked were assured of as hospitable a welcome as could
be given in the humble cottages of the wreckers while the booty was
being divided up.

Today, where Aydin dragged up his galleots and where the
wreckers lured ships to their doom, there are some of the finest
sandy beaches and the most translucent water in the Balearics.
Accommodation is still on a simple scale, although this is not likely
to last forever. Formentera is essentially for sun and sea lovers.
Nevertheless it is worth making the journey along Formentera's
principal road to the east end of the island because of its wonderful
views. The first village after leaving San Francisco is San Fernando,
an untidy collection of houses from where a track in a poor state
of repair leads to Es Pujols. The road runs approximately due east,
keeping more and more to the north shore as far as Es Calo: to
its south there is arable and pasture land with thickets of pine
beyond, through which run several tracks down to the Playa de
Mitjorn.

After leaving Es Calo, of which there is very little to see, the
road turns south and starts to climb towards Mola, the island's
loftiest point, 600 feet high; Mola in Catalan means 'hill' or 'high
place'. After some fairly sharp bends, the road resumes its easterly
direction and, after passing mature pinewoods, reaches the little
village of Nuestra Señora del Pilar, the island's most easterly
hamlet. Here is a community of scattered farms round a dazzling
white church of recent construction after which the place is named.
On this plateau, which stretches as far as the lighthouse at the
island's eastern end and for a considerable distance on either side
of the road, there is excellent farming country. Sheep and cows

graze in the fields, the arable land produces bountiful crops and vines flourish, protected by drystone walls.

There are usually light breezes in summer—this is part of the island's charm—but in the first months of the year there are winds, which can blow hard and steadily from the north-west. Solitary trees standing in fields, and those on the northern or western fringes of the woods, have been battered into the most extraordinary shapes as a result of the wind's domination during winter and spring. Fig trees grow sideways rather than upwards, just as they do in the western parts of Ibiza, and the branches are supported by innumerable crutches. It is when these winds drop that summer begins to stir.

At the point where the road starts its descent from the eastern plateau back towards San Francisco Javier there is a most spectacular view of Formentera and of distant Ibiza beyond. The middle and western part of the island are spread out below like a carpet. On the south side the long, sandy beach backed by woods of the Playa de Mitjorn extends as far as the Torre Catala where it is replaced by the steep green slopes stretching down to Cabo Berberia, the island's most southerly point, where low cliffs fall to the sea. There are also sandy beaches on the north shore where the coastline can be seen as far as the Punta Prima, behind which, invisible, lies the Playa d'es Pujols. To the north-west lies Ibiza with its mountains. At its most westerly visible point lies Es Vedra, standing out to sea like a great galleon. On Ibiza's eastern side is the rugged, indented coast leading as far as the islet of Tagomago. Figueretas, Talamanca and Cala Llonga with their recently built hotels can be clearly seen. It is a breathtaking view when visibility is good.

Part Two

MINORCA

⚜ 10 ⚜

A General Survey

Some 135 miles north-east of Ibiza, and on the far side of Majorca, lies Minorca, with its own quiet, distinctive individuality. Ibiza is the smallest of the three main islands in the Balearic group, but Minorca has perhaps been the remotest, especially as it is further away from Madrid, the Spanish capital, than any other part of Spain. This isolation was particularly noticeable during the 55 years following the capture of the island by James I of Aragon in 1232 when the inhabitants of Minorca acknowledged the Christian king as their overlord, but themselves remained Muslim.

Minorca is approximately 30 miles long from east to west, some 12 miles across at its widest point and has a coastline of over 135 miles. Geologically, it is partly linked with the Miocene lime-stone of the Tertiary period, the same that is to be found in Ibiza and Majorca, and is therefore a continuation of the mountains of Andalusia. A third of the island on the north side is predominantly Devonian, however, a much harder stone, and corresponds with the mountains of Catalonia and their extensions in southern Provence.

The division of Minorca into two distinctive geological sectors makes for two very different sorts of countryside. The highest point of the island, Monte Toro, which rises to 1,206 feet, is almost exactly halfway between Ciudadela and Mahon and between the north and south coasts. A view of the north from its upper slopes reveals rolling open countryside with occasional high ground extending to the distant rugged shoreline, indented with little sandy coves and the great inland Bay of Fornells. There are few houses and few exposed stones to be seen. The meagre grass is occasionally shadowed by clumps of ilex and the wild olive, while here and there stretches of pinewood spread over the verdant hillside. The only village of any size is Fornells.

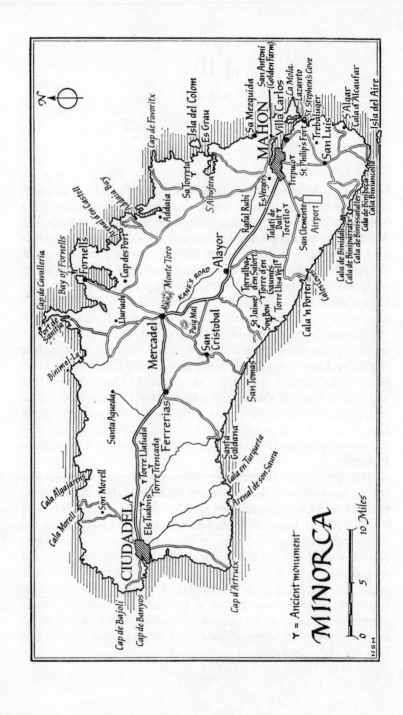

MINORCA

Y = Ancient monument

0   5   10 Miles

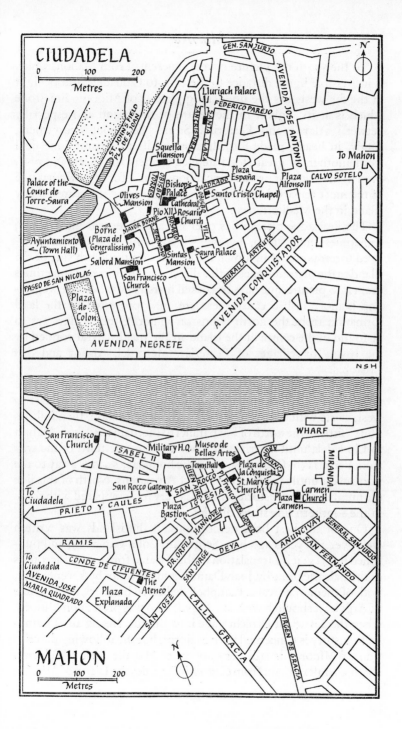

CIUDADELA

0 100 200
Metres

GEN. SAN JURJO

Lluriach Palace

FEDERICO PAREJO

AVENIDA JOSE ANTONIO

To Mahon

CALVO SOTELO

ST. JOHN'S FIELD
PLA. DE S. JUAN

SANTA CLARA

SAN CRISTOFOL

Squella
Mansion

Plaza
España

Plaza
Alfonso III

QUADRADO

OBISPO

Palace of the
Count de
Torre-Saura

Olives
Mansion

Bishop's
Palace

Cathedral

Santo Cristo Chapel

OBISPO VILA

Pio XIII

Rosario
Church

Borne
(Plaza del
Generalissimo)

MAYOR BORNE

SEMINARIO

ROSARIO

Ayuntamiento
← (Town Hall)

Salord Mansion

Sintas
Mansion

Saura Palace

MURALLA ARTRUX

AVENIDA CONQUISTADOR

San Francisco
Church

PASEO DE SAN NICOLAS

Plaza
de
Colon

AVENIDA NEGRETE

NSH

WHARF

San Francisco
Church

ISABEL II

Military H.Q.

Museo de
Bellas Artes

To
Ciudadela

San Rocco Gateway

Town Hall

BUEN AIRES

Plaza de
la Conquista

St. Mary's
Church

ARDANA

MIRANDA

Carmen
Church

Plaza
Carmen

PRIETO Y CAULES

SAN ROCCO

Plaza
Bastion

IGLESIA

P. FRANCO

GEN. LOPEZ

RAMIS

HANNOVER

ANUNCIVAY

GENERAL SAN JURJO

SAN FERNANDO

To
Ciudadela

AVENIDA JOSE
MARIA QUADRADO

CONDE DE CIFUENTES

DR. ORFILA

The
Ateneo

SAN JORGE

DEYA

SAN JOSE

Plaza
Explanada

CALLE GRACIA

VIRGEN DE GRACIA

MAHON

0 100 200
Metres

N

To the south the picture is very different. From Mahon, which is just visible in the distance to the east, to Ciudadela, out of sight in the far west, lies the undulating plateau of Miocene limestone which is at its highest in the centre of the island and especially between Alayor and Ferrerias. Stones lie about everywhere, singly, in heaps, made into drystone walls to separate one field from another, in great stone-stepped shelters for sheep and pigs, even in the shape of pre-historic monuments—for Minorca has one of the most remarkable collections of prehistoric structures of any island in the Mediterranean.

The limestone plateau has over the ages been cut into valleys, sometimes quite steep, by the winter rains which form brief-lived torrents tumbling down into the sea on the south side of the island as the plateau slopes in this direction. The torrents sometimes drain into picturesque bays or coastal marshland where the vegetation is more lush because these are areas protected by the land formation from the north winds of winter. Other valleys are to be found in the centre of the island in the quadrilateral formed by the towns or villages of Ferrerias, Mercadel, Alayor and San Cristobal.

A broad dividing line between the limestone of the south and the predominating Devonian rock of the north, running from east to west, starts with the great natural harbour of Mahon, then follows a line a little to the north of but parallel to the main road from Mahon to Ciudadela until it arrives at a point about one-third of the way from Ferrerias to Ciudadela. Here the boundary swings away to the north-west until it ends in the Bay of Algaiarens. North of this line the number of pre-historic remains is very few compared with those in the southern limestone district.

One of the best brief descriptions of the islands was written well over 250 years ago by a Scotsman, Colin Campbell, and published in 1715: it is a translation in abbreviated form of two accounts of the Balearics, one by Juan Dameto and the other by Vicente Mut, both of them Majorcans. Campbell dedicated his work to the Duke of Argyle (it should have been Argyll) who was present on Minorca when the Treaty of Utrecht gave it to Britain. Nearly all of Campbell's history is concerned with Majorca, but the following description of Minorca is still very apposite: 'To the East of *Majorca*, about 30 miles distant from *Cape de la Pera*, lies the Island of *Minorca*.

The Land is partly plain and partly mountainous; tho' its Hills are neither so high nor so fruitful as those of the other Island, yet it wants none of the Necessaries of Life. There are here both great and small Cattel; from which they make Butter and very good Cheese. Its being exposed to the excessive Colds of the North, is the reason that it is destitute of Oyl. The Climate, Language, Manners and everything else are the same with those of the greater Island, with the difference, that it is neither so rich nor so populous.'

That Minorca is 'neither so rich nor so populous' is mainly due to the climate which is much more severe during the winter than it is in Majorca and Ibiza. It lies especially exposed to the north winds, or *tramontana*, which blow intermittently from October to April southwards down the River Rhône across the cold blue waters of the Mediterranean to the island's open northern shore. Unlike Majorca, there is no barrier of mountains to act as a protection for the rest of the island. The *tramontana*, usually a dry wind, can reach gale proportions during winter: in Mahon they may be twice as strong as those experienced in Palma, Majorca, where the annual mean rainfall of 18 inches compares with 24 inches in Mahon. The choice of the olive on occasion to symbolize the island—the wild olive, not the fruit-producing variant—is probably because of its tenacity, bending but not breaking under the pounding winds of winter, and its ability to sink its roots deep into the soil in the cracks in the rocks and cling on. In summer, the blue skies and the sea are as idyllic as anywhere in the Mediterranean.

The inhabitants are of similar, although perhaps not exactly the same stock, as the Majorcans, as Colin Campbell suggests. Both islands were occasionally visited by Greeks and Carthaginians, followed in turn by Romans, Vandals, Byzantines and Muslims who came as settlers, until the last were largely swept away by the victorious and acquisitive Catalans in the thirteenth century. Minorca however alone underwent British rule, starting in 1708 and lasting for 71 years in three stages until 1802. In addition there was a brief French occupation in mid-century from 1756 to 1763. Gaston Vuillier wrote in the 1890s, 'In the streets I often met quite English faces, little girls with fair hair and blue eyes, and young men with chestnut hair.' There was not, however, much marriage between the established island families and members of the British forces, although the latter were not unacceptable as companions, judging by the following somewhat arch passage taken from *The History of the Island of Minorca* by John Armstrong. This was written in the form of a series of letters to Brigadier-General Richard Offarrell to whom the book, published in 1752, was dedicated. In this passage, Armstrong wrote: 'It I were not to mention the Ladies, a Gentleman of your gallantry would have cause to be offended. In the commerce with them, two things are requisite, an open Hand, and a close Mouth, and I venture to say, little else is necessary here to accomplish a successful Lover, or what the *French* call *Un homme à bonnes fortunes.*'

John Armstrong, who described himself as 'Engineer in ordinary to His Majesty', much enjoyed his years on the island. He was highly observant as is evident in his book, which he compiled to pass away the time. The Minorcans he found a sober people, in marked contrast to the rank and file of the British army and navy in those days. 'When a Spaniard broaches a Butt of wine, he has two soldiers sent him by the Commanding Officer, to see that no Disorders are committed in the *Bota-fresca* House and a Green Bush is hung out at the door, as was formally the Practice in England; whence the Proverb, *Good Wine needs no Bush.* . . . Hither the soldiers repair, to regale themselves, and such of the Seamen as are on the Shore. . . . In the Temple of Bacchus, no bounds are set to their Debauches and such a Quantity of Wine is daily swallowed down, as would stagger Credulity itself to be told of it.'

The land was not so well cared for then by its farmers as it is today. During the British occupation, a third of its wheat requirements and all of its oil had to be imported, according to Armstrong. He noted the many opportunities open to the Minorcans—the growing of cotton, oil and tobacco, fishing and so on—but found the inhabitants exceptionally indolent. Perhaps they were cursed with the malarial mosquito, which has afflicted so many other parts of the Mediterranean—Armstrong himself mentions the prevalence of the mosquito or gnat—or perhaps there was no one to help them do new things by teaching new methods. They did however take good care of their vineyards, much to the delight of the British forces. André Grasset de St. Sauveur, the French consul in the Balearic Islands at the beginning of the nineteenth century, also noted in his book on the Balearics that the Minorcan wines were excellent, equal to good burgundy. Only a little wine is produced today and that in the San Luis area: unfortunately, nearly all the vineyards were ruined by phylloxera, the vine pest, at the end of the last century.

If, in Armstrong's day, the Minorcans were sober and indolent, today they are sober and industrious, good-humoured and friendly, if somewhat reserved, as may be expected from a basically Catalan people. They are practical and down to earth, and very ready to take up the opportunities that tourism and other activities have brought them in recent years. These changes can be seen everywhere. On the land, intensive cattle rearing is replacing cereal farming: the milk is used for making Minorca's famous Mahon cheese which, together with beef, is exported in considerable quantities. Ploughing and reaping are now mechanized. The Minorcans are however still strongly regionalist by tradition and speak and write a version of Catalan, not Castilian, among themselves.

There has been a trend away from the land to take up work in the towns. For the last hundred years the making of shoes has been a major industry, followed in importance by fancy jewellery: these two activities occupy 70 per cent of the island's labour force, because they pay more than agriculture. Many families have their own television set, refrigerator and car. Minorca is coming into line with the standards of European industrial society. This in turn means more growth in the towns. Both in Mahon and in Ciudadela, new houses and small apartment blocks have spread everywhere. Building is also beginning to take place along the coast.

The latest industry to reach Minorca is tourism. This started in earnest with the recent construction of an airport capable of taking modern jet aircraft. The recent hotel and villa building boom dates from about this time. Before this only one or two hotels had accommodated tourists. In still earlier days, the inns were of the simplest in every sense and scarcely encouraged visitors to come to Minorca. Today, standards of food and comfort are the same as elsewhere in Spain. Some 20 hotels have been built in the last few years, many of them to a high standard of design. One or two hauntingly beautiful sites have, however, been ruined visually because the buildings erected there are in size quite out of proportion with their surroundings. This could be the fate of more areas of outstanding scenic quality if the present pace of building hotels and villas continues. One hopes that substantial stretches of coast-line will remain undeveloped or declared a nature reserve as a means of ensuring that this beautiful island maintains its charm and continues to attract visitors.

11

Prehistoric Minorca

Minorca has been called the island of wind and stones. The wind's work, if only felt during the winter, is evident throughout the year, in the twisted shape of the trees. In the brilliant summer sunshine they are a reminder that winter will return. The stones are everywhere, at least in the southern and western parts of the island. The traveller leaving the airport will immediately be impressed by the numbers of grey limestone boulders piled together in the corners of fields, or formed to make a guard round a tree, or built into a drystone wall. Stones which have recently been uprooted are occasionally faintly stained a pale terracotta or a reddish brown from the soil in which they have lain: exposure for any length of time however seems to kill any trace of warmth in the colour, leaving them cold, grey and lifeless.

The drystone walls are still built today according to the Cyclopean or megalithic techniques of Mycenae and Tiryns. These same methods were also used to build the towers of stones which are to be found scattered about the island, towers which are known in Minorca as *talayots*, and were raised by peoples who settled in Majorca and Minorca during the Bronze Age or in the second millennium B.C., bringing with them a knowledge of this type of structure. We have very little definite information about the origins of these peoples. Similar megalithic structures have been found throughout the eastern Mediterranean; in particular, resemblances between the *talayots* of Minorca and the *nuraghi* and 'giant' tombs of Sardinia suggest that Minorca may have been colonized from there. But it is doubtful that we shall ever be certain of the answer to this question. This megalithic building probably continued in Minorca and Majorca even after the islands were occupied by the Romans following their conquest of Majorca in 123 B.C.

Both islands are rich in monuments of the Cyclopean or Talayot period, but Minorca enjoys a far greater number. Moreover, those of Minorca do not appear to have deteriorated as much as those of Majorca, although many have been destroyed in both, even in recent years, because of the local demand for dressed stone. One further point of comparison between the two islands should be made: the monuments of Minorca often show more inventiveness and greater boldness in design than those of the larger island. Perhaps Majorca was more isolated because it was further west than Minorca and therefore less in touch with Italy, Greece and Egypt where the main trends in architectural design during this remote prehistoric period seem to have originated. Furthermore, there were in Minorca such structural forms as *taulas* and *navetas* which have not yet been discovered in Majorca.

Looking at the Minorcan countryside, it is often extremely difficult to decide which pile of stones is modern and which pre-historic. There are, moreover, practical difficulties in finding out. The holm-oak, wild olive and every kind of thorned and spiked shrub growing in the Mediterranean seem to make these heaps of stones, ancient or modern, particularly their own. To the farmers, the clearing of stones from their workable fields is essential, but to remove trees and undergrowth from the piles of stones in the hope that a previously unknown Talayotic site may thus be un-covered is another matter. The roots of these trees sink deeply and their eradication can be a time-consuming and expensive business.

Because of the rugged nature of the countryside, it is extremely difficult to pinpoint exactly the position of a specific monument. There are good local maps, and one in particular marks by symbols the positions of various types of prehistoric structure, but these are only approximations. On reaching the neighbourhood of the monument in question, 'no trespassing' notices may be in evidence, because the local landowner does not wish unknown visitors to tramp over his property and write their names on his prehistoric treasures: such notices however are not very frequently seen. A vantage point must first be found from which to scan the surround-ing area for the object of the search, which may be a *talayot* or a village enclosure, but the presence of a great many stones, some-times heaped into a large pile or built up to form a wall, probably of recent origin, does not simplify the task of identification. The seeker may well be successful in identifying his monument, only to find that a wall, hidden by a fold in the ground which also shields a quite impassable ravine filled with an impenetrable tangle of evergreen shrubs, lies between himself and it. There are however excellent examples of the more important forms of prehistoric structure which can be visited without difficulty.

Over 1,600 prehistoric monuments are known to exist in Minorca, of which only a comparative few have been excavated. More may well be discovered in the future. The period of the Talayot culture does not cover all the centuries of prehistoric man's existence here. There is no unanimity of opinion as to when man first settled in Majorca and Minorca, especially when his problems in navigating the Mediterranean are considered. Until recently, scholars have generally accepted a date no earlier than about 2,000 B.C. In the last few years, however, some fascinating discoveries in the wild mountainous area around Deya, in Majorca's north-western sierra, have changed the picture very considerably. William Waldren, the American archaeologist, found a cave here containing some 1,500 specimens of the long extinct antelope, *Myotragus balearicus*. One of the Carbon 14 readings of their bones dated them as 5,184 ± 80 B.C.; this came to have special significance when human bones were found among them. Another discovery of human remains in Majorca gave a Carbon 14 reading of 3,984 ± 109 B.C. Horns of the *Myotragus balearicus* which look as if they had been worked have also been found in caves near Ciudadela, Minorca, together with fragments of pottery. While not all are satisfied that the evidence produced is completely foolproof, a date of around 4,000 B.C. for man's establishment in these islands, rather than 2,000 B.C., seems to be increasingly acceptable, especially as Neolithic man is known to have organized both trade and sea travel in Asia Minor some 2,000 years earlier still. If discoveries made within the last ten to fifteen years have considerably changed our knowledge of our forbears in the Mediterranean, it is not unlikely that further important finds will bring us nearer to an understanding of how early man evolved in this area. As far as Majorca and Minorca are concerned, an immense amount has still to be found out.

Little is known of the pre-Talayot culture of Minorca. Cave

sites, which were inhabited by man in those remote days, have been discovered in the ravines in the south and west of the island, where there was protection from the wind and where vegetation and fruit trees might best be expected to flourish. Some of them may have been used as early as about 4,000 B.C. The limestone here can quite easily be tunnelled into, compared with the much more resistent Devonian rock in the north of the island where no man-made caves have been found.

The majority of caves in these ravines and in such rocky inlets as Cales Coves, just to the east of the popular seaside resort of Cala'n Porter, may have been burial chambers. Juan Hernandez Mora, the Spanish archaeologist, wrote in 1924 that many of these caves had been inhabited but that funerary furnishings and items from the Bronze and Iron Ages were found in the smaller more primitive caves; 'never have dead and living been on such intimate terms.' Mr. L. Pericot Garcia in his recently published *The Balearic Islands*, a concise study of the prehistoric peoples of these islands and their monuments, has preferred to regard these caves as the cemeteries of the Talayot peoples. It is not known how long they continued in use beyond the Talayot period, but there are indications that some may conceivably have been used as recently as the tenth to the thirteenth centuries A.D., by the Muslims when they occupied these islands.

The Cales Coves site can be reached down a rough track off the Mahon–San Clemente–Cala'n Porter road, just before it turns south into Cala'n Porter. It has a serene and ageless beauty. The sea gently probes its way between the cliffs whose rock faces are pitted with caves to a little beach where one or two boats are usually drawn up. Many of the caves in these cliffs can not be reached because whatever footholds there may once have been have disappeared, perhaps because of the inroads of the sea. A number, though, are easily accessible and two or three have recently been converted into living accommodation: all that was required to do this was to fit a front door into the well-shaped entrance and put a flue through the wall so that smoke from the fire on the hearth can escape. Water can be provided in bottles and gas in special containers for a stove. The interiors are large, up to 30 feet long, and airy; the floor levels vary occasionally and some have small recesses in the wall. Sometimes natural pillars of rock were left in position after the original excavations to support the roof. An ideal weekend retreat! Some 22 Roman inscriptions have been discovered here, dating from the end of the second and the beginning of the third century A.D.: they are difficult to find and even more difficult to read, but appear to be connected with the rituals of one of the spring festivals. Inland, on the rustic slopes which climb up from the inlet and the sea, holiday housing is being developed. Other accessible groups of caves are to be found at Biniparratz, south-east of Cales Coves, in the hillside near Son Bou, south-west of Alayor, and at Cala Morell on the northern coast, not far from Ciudadela.

The great period of megalithic building which turned Minorca into a vast archaeological museum started sometime early in the second half of the second millennium B.C., introduced almost certainly by the arrival of a new wave of immigrants. The conditions they found on the island no doubt influenced the structures they proceeded to build. Sardinia, Corsica and Malta also possess prehistoric buildings of considerable interest; each island's monuments are different, influenced no doubt by many local factors.

Some of the buildings erected by these early Minorcans are to be found only in groups, while others stand on their own. The most common structure, of which over 200 are known to exist on the island, is the *talayot*, a variation of the Spanish word *atalaya* or watch-tower which in due course became the general name for the look-out towers erected in the Balearics and on the Spanish Levante coast to guard against the Saracen corsairs. Shaped like a cone with a more or less round base, the *talayot* rises from 15 to 30 feet. How much higher they were originally is not known as all recorded examples have truncated tops. Some *talayots* are solid and may only have served as watch or defence towers. Others, perhaps the majority, have an inside chamber, occasionally more than one, and a passageway of varying length. There is no stereotyped layout. Perhaps *talayots* were the homes of local chieftains as well as defence towers, or served as store rooms for particularly valuable items or even as farmhouses. They were not, however, used as burial chambers; several have been completely taken apart and no evidence that bodies were buried in them has been found.

The *talayots* were almost invariably part of a larger settlement, and a number of these have been identified. A typical Minorcan

Bronze Age township is Torre d'en Gaumés, which lies south-south-west from Alayor off the new Alayor–San Jaime road: San Jaime is a developing seaside resort. A third of the way along this highway from Alayor, an older road leads down to Cala de Llucaleri; when the road swings sharply away to the south west, follow the lane which continues due south. A little way along it a board announces 'Torre d'en Gaumés'; it points in no particular direction but the towering mass of ancient grey stones just to the west leaves one in no doubt. There is a path round the site to enable the visitor to view this township with its tumbling piles of walls and its three *talayots* standing close to one another, together with the ruins of what were almost certainly huts or chambers from which the roofs have long since disappeared. These houses were often circular in shape. The entwining wild olive and privet have so overrun the site that it is difficult to obtain a clear picture of what the original layout may have been. Yet an impression of something enormously old and significant shines through. There is something strangely moving about this gaunt, ruined settlement on its hill with views of the surrounding countryside and the distant sea, built by a forgotten people for an unknown purpose.

Another *talayot* easily visited is that at Trepucó, reached off a good road running south-west from Villa Carlos, near Mahon. It is a most impressive structure, so much so that, to overawe the islanders, the Duc de Crillon, who commanded the Franco-Spanish force which seized the island from the British in 1781–82, had guns mounted on the *talayot* and a thick defensive star-shaped wall built round it which still stands. The stones for this wall were undoubtedly taken from other *talayots* in the neighbourhood. Trepucó was the site of a settlement and in *Cambridge Excavations in Minorca*, which appeared in 1932, Miss Margaret Murray, whose autobiographical *First Hundred Years* was published in 1963, described in detail the work carried out here under the auspices of the Cambridge Museum of Ethnology.

Undoubtedly the most evocative monument at Trepucó is the *taula* which, as its name implies, is a table (from the Latin *tabula* and the Spanish *tabla*); as Miss Murray has pointed out, 'it consists of a slab of stone set upright in a groove in the flat rock floor, supporting another slab which lies horizontally upon it.' There are several facts which can be given about these *taulas*. They are unique to Minorca, although the possibility that an attempt to imitate them was made at a later date at Almallutx near Escorca in Majorca cannot completely be ruled out. They are found in settlements invariably including *talayots*, and standing inside an enclosure usually of horseshoe shape, never exactly in its centre but at an angle a little towards the north wall. Thirty-one have been identified altogether; seven are still complete, and three have been completely destroyed. Their measurements vary somewhat: the one at Trepucó, standing over twelve feet high, is the tallest; several are over nine feet, and one or two rather smaller.

The purpose of the *taula* is not known, although many theories, some more fantastic than others, have been forthcoming ever since an interest in these strange structures first began to develop in the eighteenth century. John Armstrong thought they were sacrificial altars and of Celtic origin; this theory was supported by Dr. Juan Ramis y Ramis, the author of the first study of Minorca's prehistory in Spanish published in 1818, who claimed that the sacrifices made were human. These theories were rejected by later scholars on the commonsense grounds that it would be impossible for a priest to carry out the sacrifice, even if the victim could have been placed in position, when the table was about twice the height of an average man. Instead, a more practical suggestion was made that the *taula* was a central pillar built to support the roof of an important meeting-place; the walls around the *taula* are however usually so low that bridging material from them to the *taula*'s table would be unlikely to stay in position.

In recent years the trend once more has been towards giving the *taulas* some religious significance, because of the care taken in their construction, their siting in the settlement and their evocative shapes. 'If, then, the *taula* is not an altar', writes Miss Murray about Trepucó, 'nor a place of discarnature, nor an architectural or constructional feature, it can only have some religious significance . . . the height of the shaft and the overhang and bevel of the upper stone show that the intention was to keep the stone inviolate, so that no foot of man should profane its holy surface. The splendour of the monument, the pains expended on its erection, the care with which it was enclosed, all point to the same conclusion, that the upper stone was the emblem, the outward and visible sign, of the Deity raised up on high to be viewed by all the people.' Since then, J. Mascaró Pasarius has advanced a theory that the *taula* is a stylized version of a bull's head and its presence an indication of the existence of a bull-worship cult. Others have linked it with the worship of the sun, the moon or the stars. The true answer remains unknown and is unlikely to be revealed.

Five of the complete *taulas* are, broadly speaking, to be found between Alayor and Mahon, allowing that Sa Torreta is due north of Mahon at the back of a farm which slopes eastwards down into the Mediterranean. The farmer is prepared to direct visitors to this ancient monument which is gloriously situated, surrounded by the ruins of its settlement, amid shrubbery which seems to be under control; from it there are fine views of the sea and parts of the Isla del Colom. Torralba d'en Salort is just beside the road a few kilometres from Alayor on the road to Cala'n Porter. The route winds considerably and is bending to the right when the *taula*, on the west side, is reached. The accompanying *talayot* stands on the east side of the road and is a useful guide point. A view from the top of the *talayot* shows other possible monuments in the neighbourhood: a walk into the field beyond the *taula* shows signs of a once extensive settlement.

Perhaps the most fascinating *taula* is that of Talati de Dalt which stands in a field off a little winding lane to the south of the main Mahon—Alayor road. A way into the field must first be negotiated but, once there, the great clumps of holm oak and wild olive with grey stone gleaming through them point the way. As usual, a great *talayot* stands close to the *taula* which in this case has a second, smaller, *taula* leaning against one of its ends. Around about are its enclosure walls and what may well be the sites of other monuments, engulfed by the island's evergreen, ever-prickly shrubbery.

The *taula* most difficult to find is that of Torre Trencada in the farming country to the south-east of Ciudadela. Tiny lanes run south-eastwards from the city towards the coast in a countryside without industries or towns of any sort, once the great stone quarries, which are being expanded to provide the materials for the new hotels and villas, are left behind. This *taula* stands amid empty fields a little way from a fine traditional farmhouse. Clumps of trees are scattered about the neighbourhood, surrounded by stone walls.

Twenty-one of the *taulas* have lost their horizontal upper stone or table, but in some instances it remains where it fell. In the case of the *taula* at Torre d'en Gaumés the stone still lies within its walled enclosure in the south-west corner of the complex. The hollow that enabled it to be fitted over the upright shaft is pronounced and the work can be seen to have been carried out with considerable precision.

One of the most remarkable Bronze Age buildings in Minorca is the *naveta* of Els Tudons which lies a little to the south of the main Mahon—Ciudadela road, some seven kilometres before reaching the latter. It can easily be seen from the road and is reached through iron gates. The *naveta* is a funerary building, so named by Juan Ramis y Ramis because it is shaped like an upturned boat; he described it as a temple of Isis. There is a ground-level entrance at the west end and, beyond a small vestibule, two long chambers one above the other. These *navetas* vary somewhat in form and in Majorca were adapted for living instead of for burial purposes. The excellent condition of Els Tudons is due to the care of the distinguished archaeologist, Maria Louisa Serra, and to the generosity of the March Foundation which made possible the restoration of what L. Pericot Garcia calls 'the most outstanding monument of the Balearic Bronze Age and without doubt the oldest architectural structure still standing above ground on Spanish soil'.

There are many other *navetas* on the island, ten of them, including Els Tudons, being regarded as outstanding. Most of these lie to the south and south-east of Alayor, but are difficult to locate. One of the two Rafal Rubi *navetas* is at the corner of a field on the north side of the Mahon—Alayor road, from where it can easily be seen, just over halfway to Alayor.

A number of other prehistoric relics can be found in Minorca, including hypostyle courts, sometimes called 'megalithic caves', and perhaps intended for occupation by men or livestock; the 'dolmen' or megalithic tomb, of which there are only one or two examples; and the rock caves, of which the best is Cales Coves, already described, although those of Cala Morell on the northern coast, not far from Ciudadela, are of considerable interest. A few rock engravings and wall paintings have also been discovered but they do not compare in age, design or significance with the best that has been found in Spain.

In the Museum of Fine Arts in the Plaza de la Conquista in

Mahon is a large-scale archaeological map of the island and a representative collection of ceramics and other items found in the various buildings of the Talayot era.

A few items of this period are also displayed in the museum on the ground-floor of the Town Hall in Ciudadela. A study of all available material and writings, however, has not yet enabled the archaeologists to establish without doubt the place from where the master-builders of the Bronze Age originated, except that it was almost certainly somewhere in the eastern Mediterranean. The technique of building drystone walls and erecting monuments of rough-hewn stone slabs held together without the use of cement was known in Sardinia and Corsica, Sicily, Malta, the Peloponnese, Egypt, North Africa, and in Asia Minor; in each of these areas there are megalithic buildings not altogether dissimilar to those of Minorca. Perhaps Sardinia was developed by the same people who built the *talayots*; perhaps, as suggested earlier, Minorca was colonized from Sardinia—in addition to their megalithic monuments, there is much in common between the pottery of the pre-Talayot period in Minorca and that of Sardinia at the same time. It is a fascinating and perplexing subject.

12

From the Dawn of History to the Muslim Domination

The people of the Talayot culture in Minorca did not exist in complete isolation. There were probably contacts, both peaceful and warlike, with Majorca and perhaps with the peoples of Sardinia and even Corsica. The Phoenicians must have come across the island during their wanderings about the western Mediterranean in search of trade, but they left no records. It remained for Roman historians to write what they had heard about them. Local savants claim that the Phoenicians gave Minorca the name of Nura, meaning fire, but others are more cautious, especially as the name is also said to have been the Sardinian name for Majorca. No Phoenician remains, incidentally, have yet been found here.

The Greeks probably also came to Minorca en route for the Spanish peninsula and the mines of Tartessos, as this more northerly route avoided the way along the North African coast to Cadiz which was more likely to have been chosen by the Phoenicians. They are said to have given the name of Balearics to these islands because of the slingers they found there, the Greek word for 'to throw from a sling' being *ballein*. There was in fact a tribe in Sardinia called the Balari which may also have had some connection with the Balearics. Minorca itself the Greeks in archaic times called Meloussa. The Gymnesiae was another name given by the Greeks to Majorca and Minorca. The slingers wore no protective armour in battle, merely skins; Strabo tells us they only had a goatskin wrapped round the arm, probably because of the lack of metal locally for making armour. This absence of metal may have been the reason that the Greeks did not settle permanently on these islands. Diodorus wrote that both of the Gymnesiae had excellent land and produced fine fruit, and that the Minorcans maintained great droves and flocks of every kind of animal, especially of mules which stood very high and were exceptionally strong. None of these, however, would have particularly attracted the Greeks to the distant Balearics since they could find both fruit and livestock much nearer home.

Some fine bronze figures, in several cases of a naked helmeted warrior, have been discovered in the Balearics. The majority of these finds were made in Majorca and some of the best are to be seen in the museum at Arta, but in Minorca a representation of Athene Promachos and a figure thought possibly to be of Ulysses, which was found at San Luis, have been uncovered.

While no Greek sculpture in stone has as yet been discovered, a certain amount of Greek pottery has come to light. Of outstanding interest is a beaked jug, whitish with dark bands of colour, standing about seven inches high, which is on display in the Museum of Fine Arts in Mahon. Its character is Cycladic and it dates from the early part of the second millennium B.C.; it was found in Minorca early in the nineteenth century. Most of the pottery finds are Hellenistic Greek sherds dating from the fourth century B.C. and afterwards. There have also been discoveries of Greek and Hellenistic coins. Much of the Greek material could perhaps have reached Minorca through the hands of merchants, some even captured from Greek cities in Sicily by Balearic slingers while serving with the Carthaginians and brought back as booty. Greek contacts with the Balearics probably lessened considerably once the Carthaginians had firmly established themselves on Ibiza.

The Balearic slingers were much in evidence in the various Carthaginian campaigns down to the end of the Second Punic War. Diodorus Siculus described their importance at the Battle of Himera in 310 B.C. when Carthage heavily defeated the Greek tyrant of Syracuse who was trying to free himself from her yoke. At least a thousand slingers took part; 'By hurling a shower of great stones, they wounded many and even killed not a few of those who were attacking, and they shattered the defensive armour of most of them. For these men, who were accustomed to sling stones weighing a *mina* (almost a pound), contributed a great deal towards victory in battle, since from childhood they practise constantly with the sling.' A formidable weapon indeed. Strabo reported that it was the Carthaginians who first clothed the peoples of the Balearics in tunics with a broad stripe.

Little is known of the Carthaginian domination over Minorca. Livy described a visit made there in 206–205 B.C., towards the end of the Second Punic War, by Mago, who then commanded what was left of the Carthaginian forces in Spain. A mutiny of the Roman army there had encouraged Carthage to send Mago to the strategic area around Cadiz to take advantage of the situation. On arrival, however, the general found a very different state of affairs to what had been reported. He therefore obtained fresh instructions which were to enrol as many recruits as possible and then join up with Hannibal in Italy. He first went to Ibiza where he received a great welcome and much material support, including reinforcements. 'This addition to his strength', wrote Livy, 'encouraged him to sail for the Balearic Islands, 50 miles away. There were two Balearic Islands, one larger than the other and richer in men and arms. It had a harbour too, in which Mago judged (it now being the end of autumn) that he could conveniently lay up his ships for the winter. But his reception was as rough as if the island's inhabitants had been Romans; the sling, still their chief weapon, was then their only one, and nobody in the world can use it with the surpassing skill possessed by every one of those islanders. The result was that as Mago's fleet drew in to land, it was met by volleys of stones as thick as a violent hailstorm, so that they did not dare enter the harbour. Putting off to sea again, they crossed to the smaller island, which, though the soil is rich, was not so populous or so well defended. They disembarked and established themselves in a strong position above the harbour; they took possession of the town and its adjacent lands without opposition, impressed and sent to Carthage 2,000 auxiliary troops and hauled their ships ashore for the winter.'

It is from Mago that the city of Mahon derives its name, according to Pliny. He also spoke of the settlement of Jamno on whose site stands Ciudadela today. Pliny would have written this during the middle of the first century A.D., at least 250 years after the last Carthaginian forces had left the island. It is possible that the name of what is now Minorca's principal town did not derive from the Carthaginian Mago: it seems unlikely that an important provincial centre should be named after one of Rome's most ruthless enemies in one of the greatest struggles in Roman history. One suggestion made by Fernando Marti Camps in his *History of Minorca* is that

Mahon derives from *Maghen*, a semitic word meaning 'shield' or 'defence', a most suitable description for the town. Jamno, also by reference to unspecified Semitic sources, can be found to mean 'a place in the west', which is an exact description of Ciudadela.

At Zama in 202 B.C., Hannibal fought and lost the final battle of the Second Punic War and the long conflict with Rome was over. His defeated forces included the Balearic slingers who had remained loyal to the end; they probably hailed from Ibiza and Minorca if they were the men recruited by Mago in 206–205. From then onwards, we hear no more of the Carthaginians in Majorca and Minorca, although we know that Punic civilization continued in Ibiza. It was not until some 80 years later that the Romans came fully onto the scene.

In 125 B.C., the Roman consul, Quintus Cecilius Metellus, decided to subdue the Balearics because of the pirates who haunted the many bays and creeks with which the islands' coastlines are everywhere indented. L. Annaeus Florus, a Roman historian who wrote towards the end of the first century A.D., commented on the way the pirates kept watch from the coast and manned their ships whenever a likely prize came into view. They were even optimistic enough to attack a Roman fleet, possibly that of Quintus Cecilius Metellus. But when they found themselves falling easy victims to the rams of the Roman galleys they hastened back to shore and took refuge in the '*tumuli*', by which the writer may well have meant the *talayots*.

Although the main Roman expedition was, according to Strabo's account, against Majorca, Minorca must quickly have come under control. The new rulers of the island established themselves firmly in Mahon, which became their administrative headquarters. Before too long the town gained the normal social structure of a prosperous trading centre with the merchants providing a local aristocracy. Ciudadela, which was developed at the same time, was apparently more of an agricultural town. The Romans in addition constructed a network of roads and various military posts—for example, at Mahon itself above the harbour, and on the hill top at Santa Agueda. They also adapted prehistoric buildings at Torre Llafuda and Torello for this purpose. According to Señor Mascaró Pasarius, who has made a special study of them, the total extent of Roman roads on the island amounted to approximately 85 miles.

5a Els Tudons *naveta* near Ciudadela, Minorca

5b A country cottage near San Cristobal, Minorca

6a The Town Hall, Mahon, Minorca

6b Plaza de la Conquista, Mahon: in foreground, statue to King Alfonso III and in right background the Museo de Bellas Artes

The visitor will occasionally come across short stretches of these roads, especially in the area around Alayor where many of the pre-historic villages were concentrated. One of the most important was the road connecting Mahon and Ciudadela, and also one from Alayor to a little town and port on the north coast, called by Pliny Sanicera, but which today is the Port de Sanitja on the west side of Minorca's most northerly headland, Cap de Cavalleria. Many of the roads pass through important centres of the Talayot culture. It is possible that the Romans had decided that the Minorcans could make a lot of trouble if they so wished and were therefore taking no chances.

The Minorcans must have lived their lives in much the same way before and after the advent of the Romans. They remained in their Talayot stone villages and there began to adopt Roman ways, as proved by the many finds of Roman coins and ceramics in the countryside. Examples have also been found of indigenous round houses which have been converted into the quadrilateral shape of the Romans. But there are signs that the old ways of living still lingered on at the end of the Roman Empire.

Minorca, like the other Balearic Islands, was involved in the civil war between Julius Caesar and Pompey. In 47 B.C. it surrendered to the eldest son of Pompey, Julius Caesar's greatest rival who had been assassinated in Egypt in the previous year: the son was to be defeated and killed in Spain two years later. After this, the island, as far as is known, was at peace until the arrival of the Vandals in the fifth century A.D. When the long drawn-out wars ended between Augustus and the Iberians, the Balearic Islands became part of the province of Tarraconensis, whose headquarters was at Tarragona. A period of intense Romanization followed throughout Spain, in which Minorca no doubt had its share, with the building of new towns and roads to exploit local resources. Sanitja perhaps dates from this period. This was the time when the Balearics began to produce excellent wines for the Roman market. As at Alcudia in Majorca, Minorca also had its own theatre: its location has not yet been discovered but there is an inscription testifying to its existence. In 402, towards the end of the Roman Empire, the Balearics became an independent province.

A great many Roman coins have been found at various times, but the best collections are said to have been taken by the French

and the British in the eighteenth century, when they occupied the
island in turn. Perhaps the most impressive bronze figure of all,
representing the head of the Emperor Tiberius as a young man, was
discovered by the French between 1756 and 1763. It found its
way into the possession of King Louis XV and is now in the
National Library in Paris. A great many Roman sepulchres have
also come to light and it is thought that more may emerge as much
of the areas on which Mahon and Ciudadela stand have yet to be
excavated. Much pottery has also been unearthed and some of it
is to be found in the museum in Mahon.

Minorca is one of the richest areas in Spain for early Christian
churches or, rather, for what is left of them. When exactly they were
built is not known, nor whether they were all originally intended as
churches. There can be no doubt, however, about Son Bou which
is situated a little to the west of the new tourist development of
San Jaime. The site where the ruins stand, none of them more than
a few feet high, is protected by a solid stone wall. The church is
built as a basilica, with three naves divided by two rows of pillars.
There is a semi-circular apse in the sanctuary with a sacristy and
baptistry on opposite sides. There are no mosaics and the whole
stands exposed to the sun and the wind. Perhaps this marked a
settlement of fishermen and traders which was important enough
to be joined to the Roman network of roads.

Equally exciting to visit is the mosaic pavement of the church of
Torello which was discovered as recently as 1956. The site is not
signposted and the only guide to its position is the corrugated iron
roof which has been raised on posts high above it to protect it
from the elements. To reach the site, it is necessary to take the first
turning to the south after passing the industrial estate when driving
west along the trunk-road out of Mahon. Having proceeded a few
hundred yards along the winding lane, start looking to the east for
the corrugated roof. Another guide to the church's position is the
main rubbish dump of Mahon which lies a little to the south-west
of it—the sky above is often thick with wheeling scavenger birds
such as gulls and kites. Having located the site, there is a wall to be
climbed and a ploughed field to be negotiated before the monument
is reached. It is rough work getting there and no concessions appear
to have been made to the curious except the absence of fierce guard
dogs.

The mosaics are magnificent. The length is 52 feet and the width 16 feet. At the east end is the altar site and around it a rich decoration of flowers, animals, birds and geometrical designs. In front of the altar paces a bucolic but not entirely friendly lion; at the sides are various wading birds. The vigour and naturalness of these beasts and fowl give much delight. Close by is the quarry which probably produced the original stone for the structure, now no doubt under the whitewash of neighbouring houses.

In 1858 a mosaic pavement was found on Isla del Rey in Mahon harbour on what was thought to have been the site of a basilica; it can now be admired in the museum at Mahon. Other early Christian sites which are being opened up include one at Fornells and another close to the harbour at Ciudadela. Still to be investigated in a site on Isla del Colom, due north of Mahon.

These early Christian basilicas are said to show close affinities with the Christian architecture of that period in North Africa. It is possible that with the Vandal invasions, a large Christian population from Africa settled in the Balearics—and perhaps eastern Spain as well—which would account for these churches; they could however have been built before this, or later, during the Byzantine occupation, when the dominion of the Emperor Justinian extended not only to North Africa but to the Balearics as well.

Christianity was well-established in Minorca before the Vandal invasion. Although its authenticity has been disputed, the encyclical letter of Severus, Bishop of Minorca, about conditions on the island written in 417, some nine years before the arrival of the Vandals, is widely regarded as a highly important document. Its primary purpose was to give an account of the conversion of the Jewish community in Mahon to Christianity. The occasion for this resounding success was the arrival on the island of the relics of St. Stephen. Controversy between Christians and Jews over matters of dogma and faith became so heated that the former burnt down the synagogue after some Jewish women had flung stones at them; but all became calm once more when the latter community embraced Christianity. It was certainly a triumph which deserved to be widely known, but the letter does more than repeat this story. It reveals how the church in Minorca was organized, with the bishop's seat not in Mahon but in Ciudadela; it gives details of the way people dressed; and describes the towns and the countryside.

Bishop Severus seems to have been a great enthusiast but one who did not favour violence. Many of his ideas coincide with those of St. Augustine who was Bishop of Hippo in Africa from 387 until his death in 430. It is interesting to note these close ties between Africa and Minorca, both in ideas as well as in architecture.

In about 425 when St. Augustine was finishing his *Civitas Dei*, the Vandals seized control of the Balearics and held them for approximately a century. They were cruel days for the islanders. In addition to much plundering, there was also religious persecution because the conquerors were Arians. After the Balearics the Vandals had gone on to capture North Africa and in 484 King Hunneric insisted on all bishops within his dominions meeting at Carthage. Here they were persecuted for their faith and a number of them martyred. The Bishop of Minorca was one Makarius, a shadowy figure about whom almost nothing has come down to us. He did not return to Minorca after Carthage, but we do not know whether he died for his faith. He was the last Bishop of Minorca until the see was re-established in 1795.

The Vandal Kingdom, based on North Africa, was overthrown in 533 by Belisarius, one of the greatest of Byzantine commanders. With the dominion of Byzantium once more established in North Africa, a considerable part of southern and eastern Spain, together with the Balearics, was soon afterwards reclaimed for the Eastern Roman Empire. In some contemporary documents Majorca and Minorca are called Maiorica and Minorica; others refer to the Aphrodisiades, a name which may have originated from the time when the ancient Greeks sailed in these waters. The Byzantine occupation of the Balearics seems to have brought back peace and prosperity and allowed restorations and additions to be made to the churches. When the legions of Byzantium finally sailed away from the great harbour of Mahon to return to the Bosphorus we do not know; certain officers or officials may have remained behind in the hope of maintaining control over individual islands or areas. The first great Islamic raid on Majorca, and perhaps on Minorca as well, was in 707–708, but was primarily for plunder, not for conquest. Islamic accounts of it state that many of the slaves seized belonged to the Kings of Majorca and Minorca, but this title may have referred to Byzantine governors or merely captains of local bands. By the end of the eighth century the Byzantine eagles must finally have departed into history, for in 798 the Balearics appealed to Charlemagne, not to Constantinople, for protection against the Arab raiders whose ships now dominated the surrounding seas, and in the following year he sent a fleet to the aid of the Balearics.

For some time in the ninth century the Frankish Empire of Charlemagne and his successors was able to help the beleaguered islands. In 813 Count Armengol de Ampurias ambushed a Saracen raiding flotilla returning from Corsica and released many Christian slaves, and it is probable that the Christian fleet had control of the Balearics at this time. This situation did not last for long, however. By the middle of the century, the Andalusian Emirate of Cordova was in the ascendant and we read of Abd-al-Rahmen II sending 300 vessels to Balearic waters in order to punish the islanders for infringing an agreement not to interfere with each other's ships. Local piracy, first noted in connection with the Talayot culture, was obviously still alive. Soon afterwards there followed the catastrophic Viking raid of 859 which was probably responsible for the destruction of the palaeo-Christian churches and the depopulation of much of the island. Majorca and Formentera also suffered at the same time.

In 902 the Balearics were incorporated into the Emirate of Cordova, which was elevated to the rank of a Caliphate in 924. By the beginning of the eleventh century Cordova had collapsed, and its sovereignty splintered among a number of warring local Muslim states, known as the *taifa* kingdoms. As a result, the Balearic Islands were for over a century under the rule of the Wali of Denia, whose seat of government was on the Levante coast between Valencia and Alicante. After the withdrawal of the Catalan–Pisan Crusade of 1114, the Almoravides, a fanatical wave of newly-converted Muslims, seized power in Andalusia and the Balearics until they in their turn were superseded by the Almohades. They proved even more uncompromising but nevertheless were unable in Majorca and Ibiza to withstand the vigour, determination and ingenuity of James I of Aragon, generally known as 'the Conqueror', and his forces. The Islamic rulers of Minorca were tricked into becoming fiefs of the King of Aragon in 1232, the year when all outstanding resistance in Majorca to the Christian forces was quelled. The smaller island was however not finally annexed by the Aragonese crown and the Muslims evicted until 1287.

Minorca is singularly lacking in relics of its nearly 400 years of Muslim domination. There are traces of Islamic architecture in the bell-tower of the cathedral at Ciudadela, where the seat of government appears to have been maintained throughout their rule. There are signs of it again in a little street in Mahon called 'Es pont d'es General', and on the ruined defences on the hill of Santa Agueda, first built by the Romans, but these are in such a state of disarray that it is difficult to distinguish one style from another. There are also said to be traces of a little *Mozarab* chapel, which would have been the centre of a Christian community living under Muslim domination, at Cala de San Estaban; it has since been incorporated into the defences of the Marlborough Redoubt, built during the British occupation. Until eliminated by the Almoravides, the *Mozarab* communities were, with the agreement of the Islamic authorities, under the ecclesiastical jurisdiction of the Bishop of Barcelona. After the Almoravides had assumed power, the Christians on the island probably became slaves.

The Muslim presence in Minorca is most frequently encountered in Minorcan place names; names for example beginning with 'Al' or 'Bini' or 'Lluc'—Algendar, Binialmesc, Llucassaldent—and such places as Cudia and Canassia are also of Arabic origin, although in many cases partly Latinized. Some look for Islamic characteristics among today's inhabitants. As only a small percentage of the Muslims there remained on the island after the conquest in 1287, it is possible that the Minorcans have less Muslim blood than any other of the Balearic islanders.

13

The Reconquest

The way the Muslims of Minorca were tricked into becoming vassals of the Aragonese crown in 1232 was, from a Christian point of view, both enterprising and highly entertaining. The story is told in the *Chronicle* of James I of Aragon. The two years following the fall of Palma to the Christians in 1230 were devoted to campaigning against the Muslim forces which still held out in the deeply wooded mountains of the north-west and north-east of Majorca. No doubt reports reached Minorca of the ruthlessness with which the King hunted down his enemies as well as of his generosity towards those who surrendered. The Muslims in Minorca must also have heard rumours of help being on its way from their co-religionists in North Africa, and at the same time noted that not a single vessel with men or munitions had shown up over the southern horizon since the Reconquest of the Balearics had started.

In 1232 James returned to Majorca from the Peninsula with only three galleys. On his arrival, the Knight Commander of the Temple in Palma came to him with the suggestion that these vessels be sent with envoys to Minorca to say that a vast Christian army was preparing to invade the island. If, however, the Muslims were prepared to become vassals of the King, their lives and property would be spared. It was accordingly agreed that the King should proceed to Capdepera, high up on the north-eastern shore of Majorca nearest to Minorca, and arrange for a great many fires to be lit at night to give the impression to viewers in Minorca, only 25 miles away, that a vast host was encamped there. James set off accompanied by only six knights, five esquires, ten servants and some scouts.

'I made the galleys', wrote the royal chronicler, 'go all night with the messengers, who got to Minorca next day between nones and vespers. The Kaid [the Muslim ruler of the island], the sheiks, and the people of the country came out to the galleys to the harbour of Ciudadela and asked "Whose are these galleys?" They said they belonged to the King of Aragon, Majorca and Catalonia, and that they themselves were messengers from him. When the Saracens heard that, they put aside their arms, on the ground, and said, "You are welcome to our island; on our heads, you can land safe and sound! We will do you favour, honour and pleasure." The galleys ran their poops on shore and the men sent for mattresses, mats and cushions on which to lie down. All three messengers [which included the Commander of the Temple] landed from the galleys, besides a Jew I had given them for an interpreter. Thereupon the Kaid and his brother the Moxerif [tax collector or minister of finance], a native from Seville, whom I afterwards made Rais [governor] of Minorca, and all the sheiks, listened with attention and great devotion to my letter and message and they said they would consider its contents.'

That night, James over on Capdepera ordered the fires to be lit. They were easily remarked in Ciudadela, where the Muslims were told by the three messengers, as instructed by the King, 'It is the King with his army there: he wishes to hear quickly your answer, one way or the other.'

'The next morning, after the Saracens had had prayers, the Kaid, his brother the Moxerif, the sheiks, and full 300 of the principal people of the island came . . . and said that they gave great thanks to God and to me for the message I had sent them for they knew well they could not long defend themselves against me.' They then capitulated and agreed the provisions of the submission, which included the annual dispatch of two hundredweight of fresh butter to the King for undertaking to protect them. Then came the crunch. 'Then my envoys said to them that they had something more to do which was to give me possession of Ciudadela and of the hill on which its castle stands, as well as of any other fortresses, if any there were on the island. To this they agreed at last, though perforce and hard pressed; for after some consultation among themselves they said that since I wished it they would do so, for they had heard that I was a good lord to my people.'

The time had now come for homage to be paid to James. The Muslim party of five from Minorca, led by the Moxerif, was conducted across the intervening waters to the steep shores of eastern Majorca. Meanwhile everything possible was done to make the house, probably not much more than a hut, where the King was staying in Capdepera, look as imposing as possible. It was well swept 'and strewed with fennel, for we had nothing else to serve as rushes. I caused all the counterpanes I and those of my suite had to be hung from the walls as if they were tapestry, and I and those who were with me put on the best clothes we had there.' James was well pleased with the results reached between his messengers and the Kaid of Minorca and was obviously much impressed by the Moxerif; 'Whereupon I ordered letters to be drawn up, with my seal, which I gave them, acknowledging them as my subjects and of my successors for time to come, they in return agreeing to pay the stipulated tribute to me and mine for ever after.' We only find Minorca mentioned on one further occasion in the *Chronicle*. This was in 1269 when the King was gathering together a great host to join an expedition to conquer Jerusalem. The Minorcan contribution on this occasion was 1,000 oxen and cows, which obviously flourished on the island then as now.

The next meeting between Christian and Muslim had a far unhappier outcome for the latter. An excellent relationship developed between King James and the Muslim governor; trade flourished and the island's harbours were visited by the vessels of many nations. The same cannot be said of their successors, Peter III of Aragon and the Muslim governor's son. The generally accepted reason for the Christian conquest of the island which took place in 1287 was that the young governor of Minorca betrayed to his co-religionists in North Africa the destination of a fleet of 120 warships under Peter III which arrived in Mahon harbour in June 1282 en route for Tunisia.

Peter was carefully watching developments in Sicily where a resentful population had long been labouring under the yoke of a French army of occupation which held the island for Charles of Anjou, to whom the Papacy had given the Sicilian crown in 1268. Then, a sudden uprising of the Sicilian people at Easter 1282, known as the Sicilian Vespers, evicted the French. As the summer wore on, Peter knew that there was a possibility that the Sicilians might turn to him for help, which was why he decided to be close at hand in North Africa. He had married Constance of Hohenstaufen, daughter of Manfred of Sicily, the illegitimate son of the Emperor Frederick II. In the words of Steven Runciman in his *The Sicilian Vespers*, Constance 'was after all the representative of the House of Hohenstaufen and the ultimate heiress of the great dynasty of kings' with a claim to the Sicilian crown; Peter as her husband therefore had some legal backing when, after a show of diffidence, he accepted an invitation, brought by a Sicilian delegation that August, to place his wife on the Sicilian throne. Accordingly, at the end of that month, he successfully crossed with his army to the great island and triumphed completely over the French.

Peter was furious at the betrayal of his movements by the Muslims of Minorca, not so much because of the harm it might do him—he had no doubt told many people what he was about—but because they had thus shown themselves to be disloyal. He conveniently ignored the fact that the Minorcans were legally the vassals not of himself but of his brother, James II of Majorca. But by the time he was ready and able to take action against them, he stood on better ground. In the meantime, he had more important problems to overcome.

Peter's Sicilian adventure brought the anathema of the Church against him. In November 1282 Pope Martin IV excommunicated him and later deprived him of all his possessions. Those who were prepared to take up arms against the King of Aragon were ensured of the Pope's blessing, and the war against him was declared a crusade. From the Papal point of view it was intolerable that Charles of Anjou, who had already accepted the Sicilian crown as vassal of the Pope, should be successfully challenged by Peter who gained complete control of the island by September, 1282. The full weight of Papal authority was turned against him, and in May 1283 he returned to his Spanish kingdom, leaving his wife, Queen Constance, as regent of Sicily.

The crusade against him did not materialize until 1285. But much activity went to its making and Philip III of France accepted the Papal offer to invest his younger son, Charles of Valois, with the kingdoms of Aragon and Valencia. Philip was also able to persuade King James of Majorca to join the crusade: he was to be given complete independence should the campaign be successful. For there was no love lost between Peter and James. Their father, James the Conqueror, knew this and while he bequeathed his

major possessions, including Aragon and Catalonia, to Peter, he
was fond of his younger son and hoped he would be happy with
the Balearic Islands and his possessions north of the Pyrenees.
James of Majorca was however desperately jealous of his elder
brother and it was he who opened hostilities against Peter when
in May he landed troops in Roussillon; much of the territory in
this area belonged to him with Perpignan as his capital.

The hard-fought war went on throughout the summer of 1285.
The crusading army, estimated by contemporaries to be over
100,000 strong, penetrated some way into Catalonia under the
command of Philip III of France, but in the end Peter, employing
traditional Spanish guerrilla tactics, was completely successful
against a much larger army. His victory was marked by the death
of the retreating French King in Perpignan on 5th October. Now
was the time for Peter to plan vengeance both against his brother,
James of Majorca, for joining the crusade against him, and against
his Muslim vassals in Minorca. Apart from questions of revenge,
the two islands stood directly astride his communications with
Sicily, and in the hands of a powerful foe, such as James II had
shown signs of being, they could present a real danger. The Aragonese King therefore wasted no time and dispatched a fleet against
Majorca under his brave and intelligent son, Alfonso, who was
betrothed to the daughter of Edward I of England. The armada
had barely left harbour when Peter himself suddenly died, five
weeks after Philip III. Thus Alfonso became King of Aragon as
Alfonso III. At that time, he was even younger than his grandfather James I had been when he embarked on the conquest of
Majorca in 1229; like his grandfather, he also fought a successful
campaign. Having ousted James of Majorca, he then returned to
Catalonia. But the Minorcan expedition was very much in his mind
and most of the following year was spent in concentrating an
invasion fleet at the little port of Salou, just to the south of
Tarragona. The importance of communications with Sicily was
emphasized by the arrival of 40 Sicilian warships to serve in the
campaign. The size of the expedition later proved to be out of
proportion to the forces that the Muslims of Minorca were able to
muster.

Other factors in addition to the need to safeguard communications with the central Mediterranean must have played a part in

persuading Alfonso to act so promptly. There was his own impetuosity of character, which became very evident during the course of the campaign. There was also perhaps the hope that the Vatican might become more friendly to Aragon by his overthrow of a Muslim stronghold so close to Christendom. The expedition would certainly give valuable training to his forces, and would engage the energies of a boisterous aristocracy, some of whom would receive estates on the island. Unlike his grandfather, he unfortunately did not keep a chronicle.

The armada set sail from Salou on 22nd November and reached Majorca two days later, where it remained for Christmas. A messenger arrived here from Minorca promising good behaviour in future, but the young King, not to be deterred from his adventure, made quite clear his intention of attacking the island. Nor was there long to wait. At the end of December, the fleet started on its way to Minorca, only to be scattered by the howling north wind off rocky Cap d'Artrutx, at the south-west corner of Minorca, where a lighthouse stands today. The ships limped back to Cabrera Island and to various ports on the east coast of Majorca, including Capdepera and Porto Pedro. The weather continued stormy but Alfonso was impatient of delay and set out again with only 20 ships, about one-sixth of his total fleet. He reached Mahon harbour by 5th January where he anchored off and occupied what is now called Isla del Rey, or King's Island, to await reinforcements.

Twelve days later, on 17th January, with still no signs of the rest of the invasion fleet, Alfonso decided to attack. His supplies were probably running low and he may have felt that he dared not risk sending foraging parties ashore in case they were cut off, as he had no men to spare. He therefore disembarked his small force on the north side of the harbour, on what is now the large island of the Lazareto, but which was only separated from the mainland by a channel in 1900, and marched his men to positions in the Es Vergers plain, which lies between the Alayor and the Fornells roads, a little to the north-west of Mahon.

We do not know much detail about the battle except that the Christians, who were outnumbered by about four to one, were victorious after a hard-fought struggle. We also know that reinforcements had arrived from North Africa before the battle which should have given courage to the Minorcan Muslims. The fact is that they lost. Perhaps this was the first time that the island militia and their North African co-religionists had seen the heavy armour of a medieval Christian army; perhaps the invaders fought with the courage of despair. Some say that there was not one but two battles, and that during the second, instigated by a tempestous and unauthorized charge by Berenguer de Tornamina, the rest of Alfonso's expedition arrived, whereupon the Muslims lost heart and retreated to the castle of Santa Agueda, north of Ferrerias, in the west of the island.

The Christian army remained in the plain of Es Vergers to give thanks for their victory, to help their wounded and to refurbish their weapons. 17th January is the feast day of St. Antony Abad, who accordingly became the patron saint of the island. Alfonso took possession of the Mahon fortifications and the harbour, and set about planning the capture of the rest of the island. The only place where he seems to have encountered the possibility of strong resistance was at the fortress of Santa Agueda. The Muslim governor, however, once he saw the size of the army which faced him, decided to sue for peace and on 21st January, 1287 sent five envoys to negotiate a surrender. As well as being brave, Alfonso was a tough and on occasion a cruel prince. He had been responsible in 1285 for having two Majorcan commanders, who had held out against him in Alaro castle on behalf of James II, roasted to death on a spit, because they had insulted him during the siege. For this monstrous cruelty he had been excommunicated, if only briefly, by the Holy See.

The terms he now imposed on the defeated were extremely harsh. First of all he claimed all the towns, villages and fortified places on the island for the Christians. Any Muslim able to pay the steep ransom demanded was allowed to go free to Africa but their property and personal belongings were confiscated. Those who could not pay were enslaved and parcelled out among the various captains in the Christian army; some stayed in Minorca, some were sold to Catalonia and others to various parts of eastern Spain, to Majorca, and even further afield. Before their departure they were probably employed in building military defences in Mahon and Santa Agueda, according to Alfonso's requirements. There was little humanity or pity in the way the defeated were treated. But worst of all was the fate of those Muslims who could neither

raise the necessary ransom nor were fit enough to work as slaves.
They were herded aboard ships in Mahon harbour which, on 8th
February, 1287, sailed away into the Mediterranean to jettison their
human cargo overboard. Alfonso III must take responsibility for
this cruel action, as he pardoned Bernard Siguer who actually
carried out the crime.

This course of events must have been particularly sad for those
Muslims whose fathers had come to Minorca for safety after the
Muslim defeat in Majorca over 50 years earlier; some may have been
old enough to remember being brought to Minorca themselves.
Others may have been descendants of renegade Christians, of
whom there had been many during the ascendancy of El-Andalus,
just as Muslims and Jews accepted Christianity as the Reconquest
gathered pace.

The only Muslims allowed to go free without paying a ransom
were the governor of Minorca, his family, friends and retainers,
numbering about 200 altogether. Accounts however differ about
what happened to them. According to one story, these privileged
few took passage in a Genoese ship from Mahon to the Kingdom
of Granada with all expenses paid by King Alfonso. Another
account says that the party went direct to North Africa, while a
third says that they sailed away from Mahon but were never seen
again, implying that the ship was lost at sea.

These arrangements for the disposal of the Minorcan Muslim
population were made in Ciudadela where the king and his army
had arrived on 22nd January, the day after the Muslim governor
had surrendered Santa Agueda. Ciudadela was declared the capital
of the island under the Aragonese crown, as it had formerly been
the 'Medina-Minurka' of the Muslims. The great mosque was turned
into a Christian church where, on 2nd February, 1287, a solemn
service was celebrated in honour of the Virgin Mary to whom the
edifice is dedicated. All Muslim religious property was taken over
by the Christian ecclesiastical authorities and churches built on the
sites of mosques.

Another of Alfonso's problems was the repopulation of the
island. He was primarily anxious to find settlers of good Catalan
stock and in this he was largely successful. These new settlers
must nevertheless have depended much upon the local knowledge
of those Muslims who had stayed behind, probably as slaves,

some of whom may not have come originally from Africa but may conceivably have been descended from remote ancestors who had built the *talayots*. A procession and service is still held every year to commemorate King Alfonso's entry into Ciudadela; the image of St. Antony Abad is carried in the cortège which is led by three horsemen, one of whom bangs the ground three times with a staff to announce the arrival of the King at the entrance to the city in the Plaza Alfonso III.

Alfonso paid special attention to giving extensive estates to those among his followers who decided to live on the island and cultivate their land personally. Muslim houses in Ciudadela, the only centre at that time to boast a residential population, were given by the King to those who wished to establish business enterprises. He was overgenerous to a fault, so thought his successor, James II of Majorca, in giving land to the religious orders, among them the Franciscans and the Clares. Some in fact nicknamed him 'the Generous' and implied that he was quite capable of giving the same piece of land to more than one suppliant. He did not, however, have the opportunity of seeing the development of Minorca under the Aragonese crown as he died at Barcelona in June 1291 when only twenty-five.

14

Christian Minorca until the Eighteenth Century

With the departure of Alfonso III for the Peninsula early in 1287, Minorca sank into obscurity. The eviction of the Muslims and their replacement by settlers of good Catalan stock made an uprising against the new establishment unfeasible. As in Majorca, so in Minorca the Aragonese authorities had done their job thoroughly. But the ownership of the Balearic Islands was very much in dispute during the last few years of the thirteenth century. For in a remote, yet very real way, the Christian Balearics, of which Minorca was now one, became highly involved in the greatest of all medieval power struggles, that between Empire and Papacy.

Peter III of Aragon had been successful in defeating the crusade sent against him in 1285, only to die a few weeks afterwards. The Papacy was then able to gain by diplomacy and prestige what had been lost by warfare, and made sure that Sicily should be ruled by a King chosen by and loyal to the Pope. Peter's second son, James, who had until then been King of Sicily, succeeded Alfonso as James II of Aragon. He was successfully won over by the Papacy to support Charles of Anjou as lawful King of Sicily, even though it meant fighting against his brother Fadrique whom he himself had placed on the Sicilian throne, and against the people he had ruled. It also meant the return of the Balearic Islands to his deposed uncle, James II of Majorca. There was little love between the two and James, who should have gone home to his islands in 1295, was unable to get there until 1298. His remaining thirteen years were mainly spent in the Balearics (actually in Majorca).

James II of Majorca was a conscientious and capable ruler. Measures to safeguard the royal patrimony, to see that land was fairly and equitably held, that markets took place regularly and that trade was developed overseas were put into operation in both

7a Two streets in Mahon

7b Village of Mercadel, Minorca, with Monte Toro in background

8a The classical-styled west entrance to the Catalan-Gothic cathedral of Ciudadela

8b The Borne, Ciudadela, with the obelisk which commemorates the Turkish attack of 1558

Minorca and Majorca, and he was anxious to ensure that the islands' administrations worked effectively; certainly little attention had been paid to them during the Aragonese supremacy when Alfonso III and James II of Aragon had been almost wholly occupied with international problems. James of Majorca by contrast appears to have concentrated on domestic affairs. The amount of land to be held in return for a knight's service in Minorca was re-organized on a more rational basis than hitherto under a royal commission which took up its duties in 1301 in the church of San Francisco in Ciudadela. Every detail is said to have been recorded meticulously. The commission laid down on behalf of the King that a knight's estate should amount to what fifteen pairs of oxen could plough in one day; this was less than what Alfonso had on occasion given and no doubt protests were made. The duties of those granted estates were also clarified. Each owner had to have a horse capable of carrying him into battle when required; he had also to share the produce of his estate with his peasants. Inheritance was on the basis of primogeniture to avoid the splintering of estates. James took this opportunity of withdrawing many of the gifts handed out on such a generous scale by Alfonso to the religious orders.

Another measure taken at James's behest was the foundation of a new village at Alayor. In Majorca, one of his best remembered acts has been the establishment of eleven new island towns. In Minorca, he was administratively active in the creation of seven parishes into which the island was divided. Santa Maria in Ciudadela was the senior church and its incumbent was given the rank of provost. The other churches were San Juan de Monastrell, just to the south of Ciudadela; San Bartolomé de Ferrerias; Santa Cruz de Lluriach, north of Mercadel; Santa Eulalia de Alayor; San Lorenzo de Binixems, north-east of Alayor where a little sanctuary stands today; and Santa Maria de Mahon. It is possible that James hoped that these parishes would encourage the growth of population, but he was not so successful here as he had been with his towns in Majorca. The churches in the countryside had as congregations the proprietors and peasants of the neighbouring estates, but rarely settled villagers.

Another benefit which James gave to Minorca was the *Carta Puebla,* a bill of rights similar in scope to those enjoyed by the inhabitants of Majorca. The fortifications of Ciudadela and Mahon were strengthened where necessary, and kept in good repair, presumably by the use of slave labour. Markets were instituted in Mahon on Mondays, Mercadel on Thursdays and Ciudadela on Saturdays. That markets were being held in Mahon looks as if a village or town was beginning to develop here. The reign of James of Majorca also saw the rapid growth of overseas trade, not in Mahon, although it possesses one of the finest harbours in the Mediterranean, but in Palma where trading exchanges were established by the Genoese, Pisans and others. Mahon never even started to achieve the commercial fame and wealth of Palma.

Considering the extent of his scattered Kingdom, it is unlikely that James ever visited Minorca; at least there is no record to this effect. It is unfortunate that so many of the island's ancient records were destroyed by the Turks during their seizure and destruction of Ciudadela in 1558. Prior to this date, available information about Minorca and its people is only fragmentary but there are apparently many references to the island in the historical and diocesan archives in Palma, Majorca, on which much work has still to be undertaken. There is little doubt, however, that James was the true architect of Christian Minorca; so sound were his foundations that few administrative changes were needed during the next three centuries.

The Majorcan dynasty maintained control over the Balearics until 1343 when the problems which divided Peter III of Aragon and James II of Majorca came to a head once more. On the earlier occasion Peter had been concerned with the safety of communications between Catalonia and Sicily. Now it was Sardinia. This great island had been given by the Papacy to the House of Aragon in exchange for relinquishing Sicily. But Sardinia was only to be held by conquest. James II of Aragon opened his campaign in 1323 and was helped in every way by his cousin, King Sancho of Majorca, who was then nearing the end of a peaceful and prosperous reign, from which Minorca must have benefited as well as Majorca. There then followed an eight years' minority, until Sancho's nephew, James III of Majorca, was old enough to rule. His early years on the throne promised well. On reaching maturity, however, he started to alienate not only those around him but also Peter IV, who had succeeded James II as King of Aragon. Anxious to gain complete control of the Balearics, Peter invaded Majorca and defeated James III without difficulty, thus gaining Minorca and

Ibiza as well. The line of Majorcan Kings ended for all practical purposes with the death of James III in 1349 at the battle of Lluchmayor in Majorca.

If events in Minorca mirrored those in Majorca, then the incorporation of these islands into the Aragonese Kingdom must have brought about a general decline in prosperity. With the source of authority miles away in Catalonia, the administration became slacker. Minorca became involved in most of the disputes which beset the crown in other parts of the realm; between 1380 and 1400 there were, for example, uprisings of the peasantry and artisans against the landowners and merchants. So many of the population was lost, after the Balearics came under Aragonese rule, through epidemics and other causes, that, in 1427, Alfonso V offered pardons to delinquents on condition that they settled in Minorca. The population was thus increased, but not law and order which were further upset by the behaviour of prisoners-of-war and fugitives from Sardinia, where the Aragonese army was frequently on active service against insurrections. Minorca, because of its proximity to Sardinia, was used as a forward base for troops and supplies. On one occasion Sardinian roisterers with drawn swords entered St. Mary's, Ciudadela on the Feast of the Assumption, which was considered a grave insult.

There was always keen rivalry between Ciudadela and the rest of the island. The most important *Universidad*, or local authority, was that of Ciudadela, the island's capital. The less important *Universidad* of Mahon questioned the powers which Ciudadela claimed over it. Such was the bickering that the bailiff-general of Catalonia was eventually sent to Minorca in 1439; the immediate reason for this was a rising by Ciudadela against the governor for executing several local inhabitants who belonged to an armed band, one of several which battened on the countryside. The governor had fled to Mahon and, as a result, the two towns were for a time involved in fighting each other.

Bloodshed broke out on a larger scale in 1462 and lasted for ten years. It was primarily a reflection of the fight on the Peninsula between the monarchy and the oligarchical local authorities of Catalonia, who over the years had come to regard their relationship with the King as a contractual one, accepting the privileges granted to them by the King as their reward for helping the crown on various occasions. With Catalonia and Aragon in an economic decline, John II wished the peasant classes to share in some of these rights. In Minorca, Mahon supported the Catalan oligarchy while Ciudadela favoured the King, as a result of which the royalist stronghold was seized by the Majorcans who were on the same side as Mahon. The King was eventually victorious but the economic and social problems continued.

Another blow was the exclusion of Catalonia and the Balearics from trading with the New World according to the will of Queen Isabella of Castile who was married to King Ferdinand of Aragon. As a result, there was further economic stagnation. There was no Minorcan involvement with the Majorcan *Germania*, which attacked Ibiza, but there was the fullest suffering from Muslim attacks by Turks and by North African corsairs during the sixteenth and seventeenth centuries.

The first major raid was in 1535, the year in which the Emperor Charles V led a vast armada of some 400 ships and 30,000 troops to seize Tunis. The Christians were successful and the Muslims lost control of the city and its fortifications. Nevertheless the commander of the Turkish fleet, Kheir-ed-Din Barbarossa, showed both resilience and resourcefulness. While a pall of smoke hung over Tunis which was brutally given over to the sack for three days—each side was as cruel and ruthless as the other— Barbarossa set off to collect what ships he could find; then with 22 galleys and nine other ships from Bone and Algiers he hoisted the Spanish and Italian flags and set out on a northerly course towards the Balearics. His fleet sailed within easy view of Ibiza and Majorca, whose inhabitants were convinced that this was part of the imperial fleet returning from its victory and therefore waved it on its triumphant way.

Mahon in those days consisted of some 300 households. The town was fortified and had some cannon, but there were no troops. The Muslim fleet, with Christian banners flying and 2,500 corsairs aboard, sailed into the great harbour and took the inhabitants completely by surprise as there was apparently no look-out system. Two friars, who rowed out to greet them, managed to get back with their horrible discovery to raise the alarm, and the crew of a Portuguese caravel put up an exceptionally brave fight, thus buying a little time for Mahon with their lives. The defenders were able to shut the gates before the invaders reached them and then began to realize the size of the force that was besieging them. Messages for help were at once sent throughout the island and to Majorca. Alayor, the nearest town, managed to slip 40 men into Mahon. The governor in Ciudadela raised a rescue force, including 160 men from the village of Mercadel, and promptly marched to Mahon's relief. Just outside the town they were met in fierce battle by Barbarossa's raiders. The governor was killed with a hundred of his best men; others were taken prisoner, a few managed to get into Mahon, and the rest forced to retreat.

After this failure to relieve Mahon the morale of the garrison began to sink rapidly; above all that of the bailiff, Jaime Scala, who was in charge of the defences. With his principal lieutenants, he surreptitiously made a deal with Barbarossa to surrender Mahon to the Muslims on condition that his household and those of his immediate colleagues or co-traitors were spared. That night, 4th September, three days after Barbarossa's arrival, the gates of Mahon were opened and the town sacked in the most ghastly fashion. The Muslims then quickly departed, laden with booty and with some 800 captives, of whom little was ever heard of again. The traitors, who were known, were apprehended, tried and executed in the following year.

The Emperor Charles V, appalled at the vulnerability of the Balearic Islands to Muslim attack, decided to strengthen Mahon's defences by the erection of a great fortress dedicated to St. Philip at the southern side of the harbour mouth. The engineer responsible for its plans was Juan Bautista Calvi, the Italian who had also been commissioned to design the city defences of Ibiza. Work on both projects started in 1554, the year before the Emperor handed over the Spanish crown to his son, Philip II.

The greatest Turkish attack of all in the Balearics took place at the end of June 1558, when 150 Ottoman warships and 15,000 troops under the command of Piali, the successor to Barbarossa, arrived before Ciudadela. The armada had originally meant to attack Mahon, but had been deterred by the new Fort St. Philip. This great force had been sent by the Turks to help their allies, the French, in their struggle against the Habsburg Empire; it had first pillaged the Italian coastline and then came to Minorca from Genoa. It returned home after creating much damage.

Against this enormous expedition, which could easily have seized and held the island, the Ciudadelans had only 40 soldiers from Castile, sent under a Captain Negrete to repair the local fortifications. There were as well some territorial units and others trained in the use of weapons, amounting altogether to some 620 men, including 100 from Alayor, 100 from Mercadel, but rather fewer from Mahon which was probably still underpopulated. The defenders put up a gallant fight. Attempts were made to penetrate the Muslim lines to spike their guns, while women helped rebuild those parts of the walls which were battered by the Turkish artillery. Don Bartolomé Arguimbau, a native of Ciudadela who was acting as governor, behaved very differently from those in command at Mahon in 1535. With Captain Negrete, he did everything possible to rally the defenders. Unfortunately the building of the *Universidad*, in which weapons and gunpowder were stored, was blown up by a direct hit and Arguimbau himself wounded.

An attempt was now made to get the women, children and wounded out of the crumbling city; but although scouts had reported that all was clear on the road to Mahon, the column of refugees ran head on into the enemy. By this time a breach had been made in the city walls through which the Muslim raiders poured and the Minorcans were completely overwhelmed. Ciudadela was given over to the sack, the houses pillaged and burnt, and 3,495 people, 80 per cent of them natives of Ciudadela, were taken to the slave markets of Constantinople. Others were massacred. Among the prisoners was Don Bartolomé Arguimbau himself and his family; so devastated was the city that the succeeding governor was forced to take up residence in a cave. Details of the destruction of Ciudadela were recorded later that year by a Minorcan lawyer, Pedro Quintana, while in Constantinople at the request of Arguimbau and Negrete.

Fortunately many of those taken captive were eventually brought back to Minorca. The Holy See encouraged alms for this purpose and the Reverend Doctor Marcos Marti of Alayor went to Turkey to find the captives and negotiate their release. He also managed to regain various objects much valued by the community, such as the famous *Llibre Vermell* (red book), in which are recorded the local laws of the island, originally granted after the Reconquest.

The Saracen raids continued into the seventeenth century,

but on a lesser scale than in the sixteenth as the Crescent was now beginning to wane in the western Mediterranean. Nevertheless a fort had to be built at Fornells since corsairs were found to be sheltering in the inland bay; work started on it in 1625. Other defence towers were raised round the coast.

The Minorcans, however, were mainly concerned with local politics throughout the seventeenth century. There was, as always, a united front against any encroachment by the crown on local rights and privileges, and the task of the royal governor must have been heavy going. On the other hand, there was the continuing struggle between the island's principal *Universidad* at Ciudadela and the corresponding bodies of Mahon, Alayor and Mercadel about what rights, if any, Ciudadela had over them. Mahon, because of its wonderful harbour, was increasingly visited by the Spanish fleet and by various notabilities, and was now growing fast. Admiral Oquendo, there in 1637 with eleven galleons in case of a French attack, was sufficiently impressed by the town and harbour to initiate the building of further fortifications and to provide the necessary artillery; he also furnished Fornells with much needed ordnance. On becoming the royal governor, Oquendo stayed on in Mahon instead of moving to Ciudadela, much to the latter's indignation. By the beginning of the eighteenth century Mahon had become the most important town on the island; this was recognized by the British who established the island's official capital here soon after their arrival.

15

The First British Occupation
1708–1756

The first sign that might have indicated to an observant islander during the late summer of 1708 that something was intended against Minorca was the appearance of British naval vessels reconnoitring off the coast and taking soundings of Mahon harbour. The ships were commanded by Admiral Sir John Leake, the senior British naval officer in the Mediterranean, then based on Sardinia. When he had received reports from his various captains, Leake dispatched two vessels, as already arranged, to Majorca to meet Major-General James Stanhope and his troops, due there from Barcelona, and to help embark reinforcements from the local garrison. On 13th September the small British expeditionary force reached Minorca and on the following evening Stanhope went ashore to start his campaign.

Why the British army and navy should have been thus engaged in the north-west Mediterranean can be explained in what follows. Britain had become involved in Minorca through the dynastic problems surrounding the succession to the last Spanish Habsburg, the sickly Charles II, who had died childless when barely 40 in 1700. The two claimants to the vast Spanish dominion, which included the greater part of Italy, Sicily, Flanders and the Americas, were Philip of Anjou, younger grandson of Louis XIV, who had married Charles II's sister, and the Archduke Charles, younger brother of the Emperor Leopold I of Austria, who had married Charles II's other sister. Both Britain and the Netherlands feared the distortion of the balance of power in Europe which would arise should the successor to the Spanish throne be a descendant of *le roi soleil*, then in his middle sixties with all his power and splendour still undimmed. France was equally adamant that the younger brother of the Austrian Emperor should not inherit Spain and her other possessions. The stage was set for the War of the Spanish Succession.

William of Orange, both King of England and Stadtholder of the United Provinces of the Netherlands, and Louis XIV saw the sense of negotiating a settlement while the ailing Spanish King was still alive. One, in fact, was reached but although the lion's share was offered to the Austrian candidate, he would have none of it, while the dying Charles II refused to consider partition and was persuaded to leave everything to Philip. Thereupon Louis XIV tore up the treaty which he had signed and Philip was soon afterwards in a position to declare himself Philip V of Spain.

The English and the Dutch were united in considering it imperative that the Spanish Netherlands, which is today called Belgium, should not fall into French hands. The possession of the River Scheldt by an enemy has always been regarded by Britain as a pistol aimed at her heart. The main British fighting in the War of the Spanish Succession was here, where the great Duke of Marlborough campaigned so brilliantly. But there were other fronts; Prince Eugene of Savoy was active in Italy on behalf of the Archduke, and eastern Spain, where Aragon, Catalonia, the Balearics and to a lesser extent Valencia supported the same side, saw much fighting too and was the second major scene of operations for the British. The greatest British soldier here was James Stanhope who reached the rank of major-general before he was 35, and whose courage, intelligence and probity later made him George I's leading minister. He died suddenly in 1721, when only 48, to be succeeded by Sir Robert Walpole.

Stanhope was firmly of the opinion that the British navy needed a base in the western Mediterranean where stores and materials could be warehoused, shelter obtained from the winter storms, and dockyard repair services made available. Minorca quickly emerged as the ideal base. It was the Genoese Andrea Doria, the greatest Christian admiral in the Mediterranean in the time of the Emperor Charles V, who was supposedly the author of the well-known saying, 'June, July, August and Mahon are the best ports in the Mediterranean.' Since Britain's capture of Gibraltar, the retention of Minorca could reasonably be regarded as assured. In addition to its other advantages, the island was also an ideal base for watching the activities of the French fleet based on Toulon. Stanhope urged the seizure of Minorca and gained the support for his plan not only of the Duke of Marlborough, but also of the Lord Treasurer Godolphin and of the Archduke Charles. Whereupon he collected together 500 Spanish, 500 Portuguese and 600 English troops with siege guns, mortars, bombs, powder and shot. Admiral Sir John Leake, himself returning to England with part of his fleet after winning over Sardinia by force to the Austrian cause, left Admiral Sir Edward Whittaker with seventeen ships to assist in the campaign. Ciudadela at once surrendered and Whittaker detached two ships, the *Dunkirk* and *Centurion*, to take possession of Fornells. The *Dunkirk* was the first to engage the fort with heavy fire, which was spiritedly returned until the arrival of the *Centurion* two hours later brought an end to the action and the surrender of the garrison. The British transports and bomb-vessels were then sent into the great inland bay of Fornells for shelter.

The population applauded their invaders, joined the Austrian cause and even contributed 500 men to Stanhope's force. Stanhope wrote at the end of the campaign: 'A great part of our success in reducing this island is owing to the zeal and affection the people have for us.'

The one exception to a walkover victory was Fort St. Philip, overlooking the harbour of Mahon, where 1,500 French and Spanish soldiers, well-armed and provisioned, had taken up positions on Louis XIV's instructions to withstand, if necessary, a long siege. Stanhope, however, quickly got his troops and guns ashore. He then put his men to building a road for moving the ordnance inland to where a frontal attack could be made on the outer wall protecting the garrison and the main fort. In what might be regarded as an early example of what is today called psychological warfare, Stanhope conceived the idea of shooting arrows into the garrison with messages addressed to the Spanish troops, who were thought to favour Charles of Austria, offering them good terms if they surrendered, but in vain.

By 28th September, two weeks after the landing, the artillery had been manoeuvred into position and the full attack began. A five-hour's cannonade by a battery of nine guns, in which eight of St. Philip's guns were knocked out, was followed by a general advance in which Stanhope on horseback lead the right-wing 'exposed to ye enemys cannon, small shot, and bombs, which they gave us as fast as possibly they could discharge a load', to quote from a staff-officer's account. The attackers did not succeed that day. A personal tragedy for Stanhope was the death of his brother, Captain Philip Stanhope, R.N., who had been largely responsible for conducting the expedition from Barcelona to Minorca, and commanded the marines in this action. He was hit in the head by a bullet while being lifted by two sailors to see over a seven-foot-high wall, and was interred in one of the vaults of the fortress.

That evening, Stanhope caught a small boy from the garrison spying on his movements. He sent him back with papers for distribution to the troops offering each deserter a sum of about two gold pounds. The next day the governor of the castle sent to know Stanhope's terms for surrender and by the 30th, Stanhope was in the castle. English losses in killed and wounded were less than 50. The success was cheaply won, considering the strength of the defences; this was also Louis XIV's assessment and he accordingly ordered the French commander of St. Philip to be imprisoned on his return home.

Rivalry in Minorca between the supporters of the French claimant, now accepted as King Philip V by the majority in the Peninsula, and those who still favoured the Austrian under the title of Charles III, had become very bitter before the arrival of the British. Philip V had at first been generally accepted, but there had been the same fear in the Balearic Islands as in Catalonia, that a Bourbon monarch would favour strict centralization of power in Madrid and would therefore be likely to disregard the local rights and privileges which they cherished so keenly. The arrival in the Balearics of Sir John Leake's seaborne expedition in 1706 in favour of Charles, which gained support from Ibiza and Majorca, no doubt influenced opinion in Minorca as well. Here, the pro-Austrian party was lead by Juan Miguel Saura y Morell, a member of an ancient Minorcan family, who had proclaimed Charles III as king in October 1706 with the approval of the Ciudadelan *Universidad*.

The pro-Philip supporters had received support from the French troops in Fort St. Philip, who had brutally suppressed their opponents, hanging 23 of them, including three priests, on the gallows. As a result of this oppression, the islanders swung heavily in favour of Charles III. Saura together with his family managed to escape to Majorca, but on Stanhope's arrival there, he accepted a commission as captain in the British army and took part in the advance on Minorca. The British authorities later compensated him for the loss of his Ciudadelan home by paying for a magnificent new palace which was erected in Calle Obispo (Bishop) Vila; it is now owned by a bank.

The British stayed on in Minorca, ostensibly in support of Charles III but basically because Stanhope was determined that the island should remain in their hands. He was always proud of the role he played with regard to Minorca, and when, in 1717, he was raised to the peerage, he took Mahon as his second title. The Duke of Argyll, who succeeded him as commander in Spain, visited Mahon in 1712. The local authorities, anxious to find out who their next ruler might be, were quick to report to Ciudadela that on his arrival the British standard was raised over Fort St. Philip. The results of the Treaty of Utrecht which brought the war to an end were not known until the following year; it was only then that the islanders learned that their sovereign was to be neither Austrian nor French but good Queen Anne.

The Minorcans were probably fairly resigned to the British as rulers, except where their ancient privileges were concerned. For these they continued to fight as doggedly as at any time in the past. The main centre of opposition was in Ciudadela, the seat of the main *Universidad*. Here lived many of the island's most distinguished families, as they still do; they did not always take kindly to the British but this was usually for religious reasons. Even less did they like the transference of the island's capital from Ciudadela to Mahon. The clergy, as might be expected, were strongly against the British for their decision to put into the British exchequer church contributions which normally went to the Bishop of Majorca. The British, for their part, felt that to have allowed these funds to go to Majorca might have been regarded as an acknowledgement of Spanish supremacy over Minorca.

Both Britain and Minorca were lucky in the first Lieutenant-Governor of the island, who was appointed by the Duke of Argyll. Lieutenant Colonel, later Brigadier Sir Richard Kane, a professional soldier who served with Marlborough in Flanders and later in Canada, gained the affection of Minorcans and British alike. He held his appointment in Minorca, according to the *Dictionary of*

National Biography, from 1713 to 1720 and, after several years in other postings, again from 1730 until 1736, the year of his death. Michael Rysbrack's bust of him on his mausoleum in Westminster Abbey shows a shrewd, kindly, imaginative face, prepared to listen to reason but determined to have his own way. The island benefited greatly from his measures, which are still remembered.

Kane at the start had problems arising from the misbehaviour of his troops; these were dealt with firmly and there are no accusations against him that he failed in his duty here. His greatest contribution was the construction of a wide and straight road right across the island from Mahon to Ciudadela, connecting the two main centres with the principal inland villages of Alayor, Mercadel and Ferrerias. The road still exists today, running about a quarter of a mile to the north of the modern Mahon–Ciudadela road as far as Mercadel, and afterwards becoming absorbed by the modern road to Ciudadela. In order to finance this and other public works, and to provide extra funds for the local authorities, who had to supply the occupying troops with accommodation, wood and oil, Kane introduced a tax on alcohol.

In Minorca, as elsewhere in Europe, there was then a great shortage of food. Kane therefore set about having the marshes around Mahon drained and converted into orchards and market gardens. He also sent home for various plants and seeds which he hoped might do well in Minorcan soil, and introduced new breeds of cattle, poultry and game, all of which were greatly appreciated by the local inhabitants. He did his best to see that produce was fairly priced and regularly visited the markets for this purpose. All this, and the commercial development of the port of Mahon, began to lay the foundations of the prosperity from which Mahon benefited during much of the eighteenth century.

Kane, however, fell foul of the ecclesiastical authorities. The eighteenth century was not a liberal one and Kane came from Ulster. The local Roman Catholic church was equally narrow in its outlook, nor sweetened by the transfer of the capital from Ciudadela to Mahon in 1722. Kane, anxious that the British troops should attend church, arranged for certain Catholic churches to be used for Church of England services. He also went so far as to try and appoint parish priests and heads of convents. The local outcry at this was immediate and prolonged. Whitehall was bombarded with protests from Minorca, and, in reply, there appeared *A Vindication of Colonel Kane, Lieutenant-Governor of Minorca, against the late complaints made by the inhabitants of that Island,* dated London 1720. Kane was away for a number of years, but after holding various appointments such as Lieutenant-Governor of Gibraltar and commands in the field, he returned to Minorca in 1730 as Governor for the last few years of his life. He died there in December 1736.

In due course Richard Kane was succeeded by Major-General Philip Anstruther who was in office for three years before being recalled in 1742 to Whitehall to answer complaints made about him in Minorca. It should be noted that the British government took seriously any allegations made against its officers. In this case an attack by the Royal Navy on him for not supplying their beef requirements may have carried greater weight than accusations by local bodies about embezzlement. The main accusation against Anstruther, who was nicknamed 'red' on account of his complexion, was that the tax on alcohol was not being used on public works but going into his pocket. This seemed to have been proved to Whitehall's satisfaction as he was made to refund a considerable sum to Minorca, according to Fernando Marti Camps.

During Major-General Wynyard's Lieutenant-Governorship, from 1744–1748, the main cause of local complaint was his introduction of the press gang to keep the Royal Navy crews up to strength. As the Minorcans were British subjects, he thought it only fair that they should be subjected like all other loyal British subjects to this method of naval recruitment, which was quite unknown in Spain. Such was the local hue and cry that the measure had to be quickly dropped, but not before blood had been shed.

British policy throughout her occupation of the island was to encourage trade from which both the islanders and the British Treasury could prosper. Mahon's importance as a centre of commerce was shown by the development of a small Greek trading colony here, which at its peak was about 200 strong. Prince Scherbatov, who had been Russian Ambassador in London, asked permission for 'several Greek merchants to settle in the Island of Minorca who are desirous to Become Subjects to Your Majesty upon condition that they may be allowed all such Privileges, Libertys and Immunitys as your Majesty's Subjects do enjoy in that Island together with the Liberty of Erecting a Church there with a Burying-Place thereto annexed, wherein a Priest of their own Communion might have full powers to exercise his Priestly Functions. . . . according to the rights of the said Greek church.'

The Greeks were welcomed by the British and quickly introduced a new and lively approach to commerce. In addition to normal trade, they developed salt pans to make Minorca an exporter, rather than an importer of this commodity. They also mined for coal. From their names—Salomo, Valsamatxi, Corfioti—they would appear to have been Ionian islanders. General Blakeney, who was 74 when appointed Lieutenant-Governor of the island in 1748, was helpful, but the Roman Catholic authorities were vehemently antagonistic to the idea of another heretical faith in Minorca in addition to the Anglican church. The Greeks, although given permission to build their church, ran into many difficulties. They appealed to the British authorities; apparently, the secret opposition 'by the Vicar General and Clergy of the Island . . . have so intimidated the Inhabitants with their Ecclesiastical Authority and the Terror of Excommunication that none of them dare to furnish the Greeks with either Materials, Workmen or Labourers to erect the said Church.' Nevertheless the necessary subscriptions were raised by Greek sea captains and merchants in the Calle Gracia and the church of St. Nicholas was built of the same stone as Fort St. Philip between 1749–1754; it was considered at the time the finest church in Mahon. In November 1750 General Blakeney received a letter of thanks addressed to 'High and Worthy Gentleman, General of the Island of Minorca, beloved Son in Christ, and most deserving of our humble respect, Grace, Mercy and Health for many Years and a Stedfast Prosperity . . .' The missive is signed 'Matthew by the Grace of God Pope and Patriarch of the great City of Alexandria and Judge Universal.' It is unlikely that Blakeney realized the distinction of his correspondent.

The Lieutenant-Governor had other problems, some of them of an unexpected nature. Early in 1749, Blakeney was writing thus to the Duke of Bedford, the principal Secretary of State, in Whitehall, 'I am always sorry to give your Grace trouble but it is now become my indispensable Duty, to lay before your Grace the particulars of a Story, whose Novelty, I hope, will make some amends for its Length, as it is nowhere to be paralleled but in

Books of Knight Errantry and Romance. . . .' What had happened was that three young Minorcan ladies, all of good family—Margaret Gomila, Margarita Sintas and Margarita Alberti—escaped over the wall from the Santa Clara Convent in Ciudadela in which they had been brought up from childhood, and placed themselves under the protection of Lieutenant George Kelly and Lieutenant Roger Schaak, both of them officers in the regiment of Brigadier Offarrell, to whom John Armstrong had dedicated his *History of Minorca*. The girls wanted to turn Protestant and get married: they begged not to be returned to the convent.

There was an uproar from the local clergy. The room in Lieutenant Kelly's house in which the girls had installed themselves was sealed up each night of their escape in front of a priest to ensure that there was no access to it by the British officer or any other young male. General Blakeney in vain tried to persuade them to return to their convent; he was not however prepared for them to be sent back against their will. The two young officers asserted they were already married to Miss Sintas and Miss Gomila, but Blakeney was not quite convinced. However, married they quickly were, and Miss Alberti was then moved to the home of the 'Hon. Captain Rollo's Lady whose Prudence and Discretion is equal to her Birth'. She in her turn was soon afterwards married to a Lieutenant French, a nephew of Brigadier Offarrell and in his regiment.

Blakeney argued heatedly with the Vicar-General of Minorca: 'their marriage is as good as our Laws can make it. Now how can I separate whom God has join'd? Would you have me Ravish Wives from their Husbands' Bosoms by arm'd force? Really Sir, this would be a most dangerous Affair, and it behoves me to take care, that for the Defence of your Religion, I do not Subject myself to the Severe Penalty of British Laws.' He did however say he would draw up regulations which would make another such occurrence impossible. Within a few months the dust began to settle and the local ladies began to call on the newly-wed wives.

16

The French Intervention 1756–1763

On New Year's Day, 1756, Captain the Hon. Augustus Hervey, R.N., later to become the third Earl of Bristol and Vice-Admiral of the Blue, arrived in Mahon harbour in the *Phoenix* from Sardinia after a very rough voyage; he was conducting to a British port various French ships he had captured on Admiralty instructions. While his ship was being refitted, Hervey, in his own words, 'devoted myself very well at Mahon . . . and was lucky enough to get in with a very pretty girl, daughter of Smallridge that kept the tavern. She and I agreed very well, and I kept her all the while, and a sweet pretty creature she was.' But intelligence began to arrive that the French were assembling a great fleet and army for the invasion of Minorca. 'Casanova' Hervey now turned his attention with equal energy to the island's defence.

Throughout most of the eighteenth century Britain and France were at war on various pretexts, but fighting primarily for supremacy in America and India. The two countries had been officially at peace since the end of the War of the Austrian Succession in 1748, but along remote rivers and forest paths in America and on dusty Indian plains the struggle continued. In 1755, the British government under the Duke of Newcastle encouraged the Royal Navy to do everything possible to prevent the French sending reinforcements across the Atlantic; the capture of several French vessels led however to a rumour of a French invasion of England, one that came to be taken very seriously in Whitehall and which led to much criticism of the Newcastle administration. 'We first engaged in a war', said Lord Waldegrave, 'and then began to prepare ourselves.'

This rumour came from various sources, supported by information about movements of shipping that might give it credence. It was only later in the year that intelligence reports began to arrive indicating that the French navy minister had ordered the construction in Toulon of twelve battleships and five frigates. As the year advanced towards its close, it looked increasingly to British agents in the Mediterranean that the destination of the Toulon fleet and the army it was to conduct was to be Minorca. Nevertheless, a French invasion of Britain was still strongly suspected and a vast number of flat-bottomed boats were said to have been collected at Brest and Le Havre. A British warship sent to investigate reported, however, that there were none to be seen in these harbours.

Despite all the evidence for an expedition against Minorca, it was not until April 1756 that the British government took the decision to strengthen the island's defences and to send Admiral Byng with ten vessels to join the small squadron of seven ships, three of them carrying only 20 guns each, which was based on Mahon under the command of Captain Edgcumbe. Byng in fact met them at Gibraltar after the French had landed on the island as Edgcumbe, having put ashore as many seamen and marines as possible to help in the defence, had left Mahon in case his ships were seized by the French.

But what of the island's defences? The strongest point was the great fortress of St. Philip, situated on the south side of the entrance to Mahon harbour. Unfortunately, owing to a parsimonious government, much of it was in a state of disrepair and the wooden platforms for the guns were in poor condition. The number of British troops, consisting of four regiments, amounted officially to some 2,900 officers and men, but the officers commanding the four regiments and nearly 30 others were absent on leave or had not yet reported for duty; most of these came out with Byng's fleet, but never landed. The commander of the island was General Blakeney, now 82 years old: his next senior officer was a Lieutenant-Colonel. The Governor of Minorca was Lord Tyrawley, a regular soldier who had fought with distinction under Marlborough and afterwards served on Minorca before entering the world of diplomacy. At the beginning of 1756 he was British Ambassador at Lisbon but was sent to Gibraltar to take over as Governor after Byng's inconclusive naval engagement with the French in May of that year. Horace Walpole had much to say about him; that he was 'imperiously blunt, haughty and contemptuous with an undaunted portion of spirit', that he had 'a great deal of humour and occasional good breeding', and that he was considered 'singularly licentious, even for the courts of Russia and Portugal.'

How was General Blakeney setting about preparing to defend Minorca? By the beginning of 1756 a very clear picture of the size of the French expedition had formed—15,000 troops with the necessary transports and the newly-built squadron of twelve warships—but Blakeney appeared to be doing remarkably little about it. He was a man of great kindness and therefore popular with the Minorcans, in memory second only to Richard Kane. He could be stern on occasion but in general found it extremely difficult to refuse a request. He much enjoyed life and was afflicted with a paralytic disorder brought on by his love of punch.

Early in February, Blakeney, according to Augustus Hervey, decided to call a council of war 'and for that purpose sent to me as commanding officer then in the port, to meet at it, which I agreed to do, after settling that I should sit next the General, with precedence of the Colonels whose commissions were junior to mine as Captain of a man-or-war, and to have the honours of the guards etc.' A great many resolutions were made but none were put into action, 'from the great indolence of the General and his ill-judged tenderness to the inhabitants'. Hervey felt so frustrated by Blakeney that he sailed off to Nice for the latest appraisal of French intentions in Toulon and then returned to Mahon, determined to try and make the commander rally the island to its own defence.

In the first place, money was extremely scarce and essential if island labour was to be paid for working on the defences. Hervey urged a local government loan at 8 per cent. The Minorcans, however, took up a trifling amount only of this stock. They obviously did not consider this their war. 'Have the people of any degree shown a desire of being employed in defence of the island? Have the clergy been known to preach up and propagate to the people a spirit of heartily joining His Majesty's troops, and giving all assistance cheerfully?' The answer, in Hervey's opinion, was the opposite. He obviously thought that firm government should have been able to achieve greater co-operation. In the end result, however, it was the lack of drive among the defenders which brought about the loss of Fort St. Philip.

On 10th April, four days after Byng had started from Spithead on the long journey south to Gibraltar and on into the Mediterranean, the French expedition left Toulon. A week later Minorca came into view and that evening the first troops were landed, although not where originally planned. The naval commander, the Marquis de la Galissonnière, and the overall commander of the expedition, the Duc de Richelieu, both seasoned campaigners, were anxious to land the army as close to Fort St. Philip as possible and had contemplated either Aire Island (Isla del Aire) at the south-eastern tip of the island, or Fornells on the north coast. Instead they found themselves off Ciudadela, already evacuated by Colonel Rich's regiment, whose withdrawal had been marked by plundering and drinking which lost the defenders many friends among the local population. That night, 17th April, the Duc de Richelieu attended church in Ciudadela and afterwards received the allegiance of the local officials and clergy. British troops were now concentrating on Fort St. Philip. Byng was not to arrive in Gibraltar until 2nd May.

Hervey was not the only critic of General Blakeney's dilatoriness. Another was a Major Cunninghame R.E. who had left Minorca earlier that year to join another regiment in North America. However, he was still in Genoa in February where he was so impressed by what he learned of French intentions against the island that he returned there with 3,000 palisades, shipped at his own expense, to strengthen the defences. He was critical of the command for not taking steps to obtain clearer fields of fire from Fort St. Philip, for failing to deny many things such as shelter and water to the enemy before the start of the siege, and for omitting to rid the Fort of unnecessary mouths to feed. The French made good use of the many supplies they found in Mahon which Blakeney, if he had been more active, should either have brought into Fort St. Philip or destroyed. But not all accounts were so critical. British troops did seize all the wine casks they could lay their hands on, emptying out their contents and taking them into Fort St. Philip where they used the wood for various purposes.

It took the French a week to make their way across the island, presumably using Kane's road, where not broken up, and to take up positions round the Fort. Minorcans were employed to repair the roads that the British had destroyed, but the heavy cannon had to be shipped by sea from Ciudadela to the vicinity of the Fort.

One contemporary account described how General Blakeney 'dispatched the Drum Major of Colonel Cornwallis's Regiment in Military Form, to demand the Reason of the *French King's* Troops landing in a hostile manner in His Majesty's Island of *Minorca*.' 'It will not be improper here to take Notice of the Politeness and Complaisance of the Generals to each other in their turn. The Duc de Richelieu having dispatched a Drummer with a letter to our Governor, complaisantly sent him a Present of dry Fruit, who in return as complaisantly send him a Present of six bottles of *English Beer*.'

The French went ahead in a very leisurely manner with their arrangements for laying siege to Fort St. Philip, and for erecting batteries on Cape Mola on the north side of the harbour entrance as well as around the Fort. The English, who were probably equally leisurely, must have been hoping for early reinforcements from the Royal Navy. Some 800 workmen including members of the Greek community who served without pay throughout the siege, had opted to enter the fort with General Blakeney, according to one account.

The fighting between besiegers and besieged was sporadic from the end of April until 20th May; then, the pressure on the defenders was stepped up considerably and went on increasing until the end of June when Blakeney finally surrendered. The reason for this change in tempo was the naval engagement between Admiral Galissonnière's squadron, whose task was to ensure that reinforcements for the British did not reach Fort St. Philip, and that under the command of Admiral Byng.

The tragic story of Byng's condemnation to death at Portsmouth by court martial is well known. His detractors asserted that he had not gained the decisive victory which could have been his if he had pressed the attack home against the French; he had thus lost his opportunity of relieving the island as instructed. Instead, he retired to Gibraltar. The court found indeed that he had not done everything to destroy the enemy ships. The verdict, however, pointed out that witnesses during the battle 'did not perceive any backwardness in him during the action, or marks of fear, or confusion . . . and from other circumstances, the Court do not believe that his misconduct arose either from cowardice or disaffection; and do therefore unanimously think it their duty most earnestly to recommend him as a proper object of mercy.'

The dice had been loaded against Byng from the beginning. A proportion of his ships needed repairs and careening when he took them over at Portsmouth but time did not permit this, while on arriving at Gibraltar he found the dockyard bereft of stores and in a tumbledown condition. He was short of crews and many of the men on deck had been rounded up by the press gangs only just in time to be sent on this expedition. Moreover, Admiralty instructions for the line of battle and regarding communications between the fleet proved highly inadequate. When he went into action against Galissonnière he found himself outpaced and outgunned by the French. A convincing case in Byng's favour has been made by Dudley Pope in his book, *At 12 Mr. Byng was shot* . . .

It was the French who disengaged and retreated from the battle but it was Byng, with the agreement of his second-in-command, Rear-Admiral Temple West, and other senior officers, who decided to return to Gibraltar to get treatment for his sick and wounded and obtain refits for his ships. Neither he nor his colleagues thought that the British fleet could have raised the siege without landing a large British force. Yet it could be argued that if the British navy had set up a blockade, the French army on Minorca might have been starved of reinforcements and supplies over a period.

Byng was to die on 14th March, 1757; in the opinion of some a sacrificial victim offered to the public for the Newcastle administration's loss of Minorca through incompetence and because of George II's determination that he should be punished for cowardice, a trait which the King is thought himself to have shown on more than one occasion. There have always been strong feelings both for and against Byng, but hardly any have approved his execution. One of the best accounts of this action was entered in his Journal by Augustus Hervey.

Admiral Byng's fleet had come in sight of Fort St. Philip on 19th May, 1756. The navy at once tried to make contact with the defenders of St. Philip; more belatedly the army followed suit, but both failed. Augustus Hervey was dispatched with two other frigates under his command to deliver a message for General Blakeney from Admiral Byng. He managed to get as far as Aire Island when he was suddenly becalmed, but was towed close enough to Fort St. Philip to see that the British colours were still flying on the castle. He did not get any further because the enemy fleet had by now come into sight and he was recalled with his small force to rejoin the main body.

Apparently no one in Fort St. Philip thought of taking any action to contact the navy except for Robert Boyd, the storekeeper, who early that morning volunteered to Lieutenant-Colonel Jefferies to be rowed out with messages. The matter was not discussed until the afternoon meeting of the council of war when it was agreed that Boyd should take a letter to Admiral Byng. By the time the boat was made ready it was only a short time to sundown. Boyd tried to reach the fleet but it had sailed on and he was in danger of being captured by two small French craft who were edging their way towards him. He got back to Fort St. Philip only with difficulty. The next the defenders knew of events was on 22nd May when much cheering was heard in the French camp because, so it was reported, of a French naval victory.

The Duc de Richelieu was delighted with the disappearance of the British squadron. It meant that there would now be no interruption in the arrival of reinforcements and supplies. He had hoped to take Fort St. Philip by surprise and had considered his force of 15,000 inadequate to undertake a siege. But now his artillery was all the time building up in strength and although the British gunners enjoyed considerable success in putting the French cannon out of action, he was able to replace them with new pieces and to construct fresh batteries. From 6th June onwards, the French artillery increasingly gained the ascendancy. The British on the other hand had growing difficulty in maintaining contact with its units in the Marlborough Redoubt on the far side of St. Stephen's cove.

On 14th June, the British made a sortie and spiked many French guns; unfortunately they advanced too far and many were taken prisoner, thus reducing considerably the number of the defenders. Richelieu therefore decided to attack on 27th June; by this time the British appeared to have lost most of their artillery and to be dependent upon mortars. The French maintained a continuous cannonade throughout the previous two days. They then advanced at night with great bravery against the Fort and the Marlborough Redoubt, but were only able to capture two outworks, with considerable losses. Soon after daybreak they beat a parley and asked leave to carry off their wounded and to bury their dead; they are also said to have used this break to introduce more French

troops into the outworks, in which they now considerably outnumbered the British.

At this juncture Blakeney called a council of war at which capitulation was discussed and finally agreed. Major Cunninghame
however was against surrender as the French had only penetrated
the outer defences with great loss. Other accounts say that Blakeney
never stirred from the central keep throughout the siege, that he
had to be pulled out of bed when the French started to attack and
gave no orders throughout the action. Nevertheless on the following afternoon, Blakeney accepted Richelieu's terms which were
considered very honourable, and the French took over Minorca.
The British defenders were allowed to march out 'with the Fire-
locks on their Shoulders, Drums beating, Colours flying, 24
Charges for each man, Match lighted' according to one pamphleteer
who wrote of 'this memorable Siege, where four Regiments and
one Company of Artillery maintained the Garrison, against such
Numbers of the Enemy by Sea and Land for such a length of Time
and with a Glory perhaps scarce paralleled in History.' General
Blakeney returned home to what proved to be a great personal
triumph, including a peerage for having held out so long against
the French. This reception was in extraordinary contrast to the
treatment received by Byng, who according to some had certainly
behaved no worse.

Augustus Hervey ran into Blakeney in July when the former was
sailing from Gibraltar to Minorca in a squadron of sixteen sail of
the line and five frigates under the command of Admiral Sir
Edward Hawke. Blakeney and his troops were being repatriated
by French transport; there were several officers among them who
regretted the capitulation. The British fleet sailed on to Minorca,
and, so Hervey wrote in his Journal, 'Found the French fleet were
gone, and I was anxious to know what would become of all our
blustering, and what this mighty fleet was to perform, which, had
it been sent earlier would have given the finishing stroke to France.'
Hervey was prepared to speak his mind; he was about the only
senior officer present at the battle off Minorca who supported
Byng until the very end. As for Minorca, 'we certainly lost the
most useful island to the English in a war that could be, thanks to
Mr. Fox, the Duke of Newcastle and Lord Anson . . .'

The Duc de Richelieu, having achieved his victory, returned

home to France where the capture of Port Mahon was announced on 15th July in Paris. He was received by Louis XV at Versailles graciously but—with an element of irony, possibly because he had demanded so many reinforcements. On the other hand, the *Nouvelle Biographie Generale*, having mentioned his frivolity, goes on to say that he triumphed over Fort St. Philip despite his own lack of means for attack. He is perhaps best known outside France for the 'Sauce Mahonaise' which was invented for him by his chef while encamped outside the Fort.

The first French Governor of Minorca was Yacinthe-Cajetan, Comte de Lannion who was at the same time in command of a French army of eleven battalions. In 1758 he was away from the island and his place taken temporarily, first by the Marquis de Puissignieux, who commanded the garrison, and secondly, by the Marquis de Fremeur in April 1759. De Lannion returned in due course and died in 1762 on the island, where he is buried. His memory is held in much esteem. He had, as general administrator, an ambitious, able civil servant, Antoine de Causan, who was something of a martinet. Administratively, Minorca was regarded very much as part of France. The chief court of appeal on all legal matters was at Perpignan, thus reviving a connection which had died with the end of the Kingdom of Majorca in 1349. Marseilles was the centre of authority on questions of customs and sanitation.

The French were perhaps better accepted by the islanders than were the British, basically because the French and the Minorcans were members of the same Church. Certainly in Ciudadela the local aristocracy, accustomed to the dark, sober colours worn by the British, were attracted by the colourful silks then fashionable in Paris. The French are perhaps best remembered by the foundation of the attractive little village of San Luis, so named in honour of Louis IX King of France, which lies due south of Mahon. Their brief dominion over the island ended in 1763.

§ 17 §

Minorca from 1763–1802

The purpose of the successful French expedition in 1756 against Minorca was to administer a salutary lesson to Britain for her high-hatted behaviour against them at sea and in North America. They also wished to be in the position to entice Spain into the war on their side against the British in North America by offering her Minorca. But Spain entered the war belatedly in 1762 and by the time that the Peace of Paris, which returned Minorca to Britain, was signed early in 1763, had lost heavily in the Americas to the Royal Navy, as had France.

The British were soon hastening back to what was then their only island in the Mediterranean. A Colonel MacKellar was instructed to proceed to Minorca through France, having first been briefed by the newly-appointed Lieutenant Governor, a Colonel Johnston who was not to make his way there until later. Sir Richard Lyttleton was appointed Governor of Minorca: like his predecessor, Lord Tyrawley, he seems never to have visited the island while holding office but preferred to reside in his country house at Richmond.

Colonel MacKellar reached Minorca by the end of May and was soon reporting home that Lieutenant-General the Marquis de Puissignieux, the acting French Governor, was 'entirely disposed to everything in the most agreeable manner'. MacKellar applied to the British Consul at Leghorn for six months' supply of beef as the only provisions the French had to spare were some sacks of kidney beans. At about the same time as MacKellar, Colonel Lambert reached the island with three regiments from Gibraltar. The French had an inventory made of what they were handing over: this included about 5,900 barrels and half-barrels of British gunpowder which the French had captured in 1756 when Fort St.

Philip surrendered to them. It was found to be in perfect condition.

The local authorities now sent loyal congratulations to George III for his many successes in the recent war 'which has procured us the inexpressible happiness of falling again under his mild government'. It was now merely a question of awaiting the arrival of Colonel Johnston. Lambert had already written to a friend to say he was on his way back 'to avoid the disagreeable necessity of being commanded by a junior officer on Colonel Johnston's arrival'. Johnston however fell ill and Lambert deputized for him until he reached Mahon towards the end of September.

Lambert then stuck his neck out, apparently in contravention of the Anglo–French peace treaty, and ordered the resident French families to depart. In support of his decision he argued that there were nearly 80 French families on the island, and therefore no suitable houses for the British. French imports, moreover, were coming freely into Minorca, 'making British trade one of total stagnation'. He also produced a petition from British subjects in Minorca against allowing the French to stay.

Johnston on his arrival was most emphatically against Lambert's attempt to expel the French. Those who signed the English petition, he pointed out, included many tavern keepers mainly from Gibraltar, who had brought enough beer and porter to last for seven years; these traders were the most likely to overcharge the troops. He also wanted to make Mahon once more a free port, which might attract a great part of the trade then going through Leghorn.

Johnston seems to have welcomed back the Greek community which had thrived so well during the last few years of the first British occupation, many of whom had served voluntarily and without pay under General Blakeney during the siege of Fort St. Philip. He took a particular liking to Theodore Alexiano, a member of one of the Greek colony's founding families, and wished to appoint him 'Receiver of Duty', a small job with an income, to reward him for his services to the British crown. Many Greeks, expelled by the French in 1756, returned to the island and revived their businesses, including the salt pans, to the advantage of all concerned.

The size and opulence of the Greek community in Mahon is illustrated by an incident which took place a year after the outbreak of war between Britain and Turkey in 1768. Catherine the Great of Russia dispatched a fleet from the Baltic to the eastern Mediterranean to encourage a Greek insurrection in the Peloponnese against their Ottoman overlords. En route, the fleet was instructed to call at ports which had Greek settlements to raise both enthusiasm and cash for the common cause. Mahon was one of the communities visited. Unfortunately a number of Russian sailors died from what was probably scurvy, among them the son of Admiral Spiridoff, in command of the squadron. The boy was buried with much ceremony in the Church of St. Nicholas in the Calle Gracia.

The Church of St. Nicholas was considerably changed after the second expulsion of the Greek community, which took place when the island was captured from the British by a combined Franco–Spanish force in 1782. First it was used as an artillery park or store house. Then, in the second half of the nineteenth century, it was redesigned to eliminate any Byzantine features and renamed the Church of the Conception. The handsome funerary stone in Latin, Greek and Russian, in memory of the Admiral's son, is still to be seen let into the floor on the righthand side of the nave. A few Greeks stayed on after 1782 by becoming Roman Catholics and their descendants are now absorbed into the community.

Another foreign community had established itself in Mahon under the British policy of encouraging trade. Johnston does not appear at first to have been so well disposed towards the Jews, who petitioned the Duke of Richmond in 1767 for permission to be allowed a place of worship: 'That in the same manner as is practiced in all other British Colonies, they [the memorialists] did Procure a Room for their Devotions, agreeable to their former custom, when before established in that country. That this Room being in too public a street, and they being cautious, and apprehensive of giving offence, a Room was built in a more private section, for the same Purpose. That on its being finished, an Order was received from the Lieutenant Governor Johnston to shut the same, for He did not consent to their using it, saying the Jurats [magistrates] had represented it as contrary to the Treaty. That this order being given, the Pulpits were filled with invectives against the Jews, dissuading the Natives from trading, or having any Connexion with them, which may prove of infinite Detriment to Trade and Commerce. That your Memorialists humbly by leave to suggest, that no Provision was made in the late Treaty contrary hereto and that their Neighbours at Gibraltar have a proper Place of Worship . . .' Colonel Johnston was soon remonstrating with the Vicar General against his prohibition of Catholics communicating with Jews, nor was there any further delay in the Jews getting permission to use their own synagogue.

The British administration, based on the original Aragonese organization, continued as previously. There were five *terminos* or counties, based on Mahon, Alayor, Mercadel, Ferrerias and Ciudadela. Each of these areas had magistrates, called *Jurats*, with the right of imposing taxes and reporting hardships or grievances to the Governor. These magistrates represented the four social orders—landowners, merchants, artisans and peasants; they could call a General Council or *Universidad*, consisting of 24 members, chosen annually by lot from various parts of the *terminos*; this also applied to the judges of the inferior courts. The magistrates were allowed to take an annual collection from the inhabitants to cover the expenses of projects in hand. The British had abolished the Inquisition, rowing in the galleys, corporal punishment and poll tax. There were continuing arguments about ecclesiastical interference in local affairs, with Johnston resisting the Catholic church authorities as vigorously as had his predecessors.

Relations between the *Jurats* and the British authorities were no worse and not much better than they had been during the first occupation. There was still the much discussed problem of how the proceeds from Kane's tax on alcohol should be distributed. Kane's own idea was that half should be given to the magistrates as a contribution towards their commitments such as providing accommodation for British troops, and the rest spent by the British authorities on public works. Johnston considered that the local authorities should find ways of raising extra taxes and not depend upon receiving funds from Kane's tax for this purpose.

The fact was that several Governors of the island had done well out of this tax. Johnston is quite open about it. It was agreed in 1724 that this tax be applied for public works, he explained in a dispatch home, 'but it was at the same time tacitly agreed, that a part of it should be a Perquisite of the Governor for his concurrence in laying on that Duty. This part was said to be Half.' It may be that the Governor was involved in some expenses in having this tax collected; it was also not out of keeping with the spirit of the age for him to keep something for his own pocket. Johnston, to be sure, was heavily attacked by the *Jurats* and by individual Minorcans, who took the quarrel to Whitehall, but the faults may not have been altogether one sided. Johnston was not helped by his somewhat overbearing personality, by his condescending manner towards the islanders, and by his unwillingness to understand their point of view. In this he is said to have been supported by his wife whose character was lampooned in Mario Verdaguer's novel, *Piedras y viento*, a classic of the island. The couple have been described as typical British colonial rulers by Minorcan writers, the word 'colonial' being used in its pejorative sense. At the same time, the *Jurats* seemed anxious to find fault whenever possible. The situation was in any case very different to what it would have been under the Spanish crown, when the post of Governor was sometimes given to favourites to enable them to make their fortunes.

Johnston was in fact recalled to Whitehall to answer the charges against him, and for some months Minorca was under the more relaxed Lieutenant Governorship of General Mostyn, whose main concern was to organize the destruction of those houses in the immediate vicinity of Fort St. Philip which had interfered with the line of fire during the siege of 1756, and to resettle and compensate their inhabitants. Compensation was tied to the amount of time spent there by the occupants during the siege. Those who had remained there throughout the confrontation were to receive the whole of the estimated value of their houses, those who had deserted only a quarter, and the remainder a third; no objections appeared to have been raised to this. A new settlement of houses and barracks was erected a little further to the east; called Georgetown, after George III, it became an attractive, eighteenth-century township with a vast central parade ground. Today, although nearly all the British buildings still stand, it is known as Villa Carlos, after King Charles III of Spain.

Johnston must have liked Minorca sufficiently well to return with his wife for a further period of office, so he cannot have been too heavily reprimanded while in Whitehall. Whatever had happened, he seems on his return to have been generally in a more relaxed and friendly mood. During his earlier years he had been in constant dispute with the Roman Catholic representatives. On this occasion, by contrast, he happily accepted an invitation to the consecration ceremony of Santa Maria in Mahon in 1772.

It was during these years that a number of Minorcans were persuaded to try their luck in colonizing Florida. An American doctor, Andrew Turnbull, recruited a group of families to settle in this semi-tropical area. They underwent many hardships but a number survived in the St. Augustine area where their descendants still live.

General James Murray, at one time Brigadier to General James Wolfe, conqueror of Quebec, took over from Johnston in 1774. He did much to try and convince the Minorcan gentry that they should obtain commissions in the British army, especially when war broke out afresh between Britain and France in 1778; one or two did so, but no more. It was extremely difficult for the Minorcans to regard the British army as their own, especially after Spain joined the war against Britain in 1779.

Murray was naturally worried about his garrison at Fort St. Philip which was both weak in numbers and enfeebled by tertian fever. Although immensely strong, the Fort was extremely unhealthy on account of the foul air of the subterranean defences. 'The two British regiments', he reported, 'look more like ghosts than soldiers.' At that particular stage Britain could not hope, with the limited resources at their disposal, to hold both Gibraltar and Minorca. Unfortunately, that is what she tried to do and Minorca was lost as a result.

The attack did not materialize at once. Charles III of Spain wanted to be sure that Spanish troops would be welcomed by the Minorcans. He knew well how strongly the Catalans and their kindred in the Balearic Islands cherished their ancient rights and laws. The King's minister, the Count of Floridablanca, therefore contacted one of the most distinguished noblemen in the Balearics, the Marqués de Sollerich of Palma, and invited him to visit Minorca clandestinely in order to test opinion to the idea of becoming part of Spain. This Sollerich did and was able to send back a very favourable report.

The King of Spain then organized the invasion of Minorca in co-operation with France. The command was given to the Duc de Crillon, a Frenchman, on account of the 7,000 Frenchmen serving in the expedition. The total number of troops involved was 16,000, the rest being Spaniards. Crillon landed at Cala Mezquida with his army and 100 heavy siege guns, arrived before Fort St. Philip on 20th August, 1781, and rapidly occupied the rest of the island without meeting with any resistance. He then asked Murray, who was defending the Fort with two English and two Hanoverian battalions, amounting altogether to some 2,200 men, to name his own price for surrender, which Murray rejected out of hand. There followed a six month siege. In spite of the mounting bombardment from the French batteries, Murray managed for a time to keep the sea approaches open: in this way a party of Corsican volunteers, commanded by a nephew of the indomitable Corsican patriot, General Paoli, the friend of Dr. Johnson, arrived to join the British in fighting the French who had seized Corsica against the wishes of its people.

Crillon then converted the siege into a blockade which meant the slow starvation of the defenders—and the arrival of the real enemy, the scurvy; some of the troops had been subsisting on salf beef for at least three years. By 1st February, 1782, only 760 soldiers were still fit for duty. The end had almost arrived. Five days later 600 men, so frail and wasted that they could hardly walk, emerged from the Fort to surrender.

For the next sixteen years, Minorca was ruled as part of Spain. At first there was friendship with France and peace in the Mediterranean. Then, in the early days of the French Revolution, there was war between Spain and the National Convention which led to the arrival of French privateers off the coasts of Minorca. The Spanish government therefore ordered the drafting of men in Minorca for military service. This went absolutely against the islanders' traditions. Neither the British nor the French had dared to introduce such a measure. Fortunately, the first Spanish Governor, the Count of Cifuentes, was extremely popular both on account of his honesty and the genuineness of his affection for Minorca. Appointed Captain-General of the Balearics, he preferred to stay in Mahon instead of Palma, although this did not please Ciudadela; no doubt as an exercise in tact, he declared that 'Mahon has more inhabitants, but Ciudadela has more souls.' He was quick to put on one side the orders about military conscription, and initiated public works for the benefit of the island.

One of the Spanish government's first acts in 1782 was to demolish Fort St. Philip, one of the great achievements of military architecture in the sixteenth century, on which the British had subsequently lavished over one million pounds. The danger of leaving Minorca largely defenceless was shown in the following year when the Algerian fleet appeared off Mahon. Vigorous measures were taken locally to equip vessels against them. Peace was fortunately made before the rival forces clashed.

In 1795, to the immense pleasure of the whole island, the Vatican, in response to a petition from King Charles IV, gave Minorca its own bishopric for the first time in 1,200 years—though as usual Ciudadela and Mahon contested the right to the honour of accommodating the bishop. The prelate chose Ciudadela, where the earlier bishopric had been established, in spite of the fact that the Governor now resided in Mahon.

The direct reason for the third British occupation of Minorca was an alliance made between Spain, Holland and the French Directory, when Napoleon Bonaparte was expanding his conquests in the central and eastern Mediterranean. It was inevitable that Lord St. Vincent should decide to occupy Minorca because of its naval base at Port Mahon. General James Stuart with four regiments, based on Gibraltar, appeared off the north coast on 7th November, 1798. While the Royal Navy made a diversion against the fort at Fornells, the transport ships dropped anchor in Addaia Bay. General Stewart's tactics were quick and decisive. He first took Mercadel in the centre of the island, just after the main body of defenders had passed through it to Ciudadela. Mahon, now without Fort St. Philip to defend it, surrendered at once while Ciudadela gave up after three days, with the minimum of fighting on either side. Stuart was able to report home that he had taken Minorca without the loss of a single man. The garrison was subsequently built up to about 12,000 men. Some were later sent to Malta.

Minorca was much in use in those days, and especially in 1799, by the navy, and Nelson is proudly remembered by Minorcans as a visitor. His naval contemporaries and subsequent historians have however been more conscious of his absence from the island, at a time when he should have been here. This was the period of the great admiral's involvement with Emma, the wife of Sir William Hamilton, who was Britain's diplomatic representative at the Court of the Kingdom of the Two Sicilies. Nelson came to consider it his duty primarily to protect the Bourbon King and Queen from the French, together with their Neapolitan and Sicilian territories, rather than Minorca, whither he had been instructed to report with his squadron by his superior officer, Lord Keith. Keith feared a French attack on the island but Nelson, in explaining to the First Lord of the Admiralty why he thought it proper to stay instead between Palermo and Naples, wrote 'Minorca I have never yet considered in the slightest danger, but it has been a misfortune that others have thought differently from me on that point.' Keith's assessment of French naval intentions fortunately proved wrong.

Nelson's one recorded visit to Minorca was in October, 1799, when he spent five days in Mahon, probably in the fine classical villa on the north side of the harbour, known as San Antoni or Golden Farm. His main purpose was to persuade the army to send troops to Malta, where he was trying to evict the French. He also prepared for London publication his *Sketch of my Life* which 'I am sensible wants the pruning knife.' Lady Hamilton did not visit Minorca on this or any other occasion.

There were the usual differences between the British and the local authorities, the latter fighting as vigorously as ever for their age-old rights. On this occasion, a Minorcan of some distinction, Dr. Nicholas Orfila, a lawyer born in Ferrerias, supported General Stuart. Orfila became Stuart's adviser and superintendant of the local Courts of Justice. He inaugurated a number of reforms in the local councils, earning for himself the hatred of the Minorcan ruling classes but the respect and affection of ordinary men and women.

The island, and especially Mahon, enjoyed considerable prosperity during this four-year period. There was a constant arrival and departure of the ships of the Royal Navy, often needing the services of the dockyards. The spending money of 12,000 troops must have been a welcome addition to the shopkeepers. A start was also made to the rebuilding of Fort St. Philip, although this was quickly stopped by Sir Henry Cleophane, the last British governor, a month after his arrival in October 1801. By this time it was taken for granted by the British that Minorca would soon be returned to Spain. This was confirmed by the Treaty of Amiens in March 1802. In June of that year, the Captain General of the Balearic Islands arrived from Palma to take formal possession of Minorca for the Spanish crown.

✣ 18 ✣

Minorca from 1802–1939

The incorporation of Minorca into Spain in 1802 brought about inevitable growing pains. More centralized methods of government had to be learned and accepted, there was a great diminution in trade which had flourished so well under British rule, and a large Spanish garrison had to be maintained. A general feeling of discontent arose and there were even some who would have welcomed back the British.

Events then took place which affected the whole country. In 1808, Napoleon persuaded Charles IV of Spain and the Crown Prince Ferdinand to visit him at Bayonne where he forced them to abdicate and instead had his brother, Joseph Bonaparte, elected to the Spanish throne by a group of complaisant nobles. When this became known, there was a general uprising throughout Spain. In Mahon, the pro-French colonel of the Soria regiment tried to make his troops declare for Napoleon; instead, they gave their fullest support in the noisiest possible manner to the deposed Crown Prince. The Bishop of Minorca sent out a circular letter, to be read in all churches, calling for loyalty to the Spanish royal family. The military governor, the Marqués de Palacios, received an order to proclaim Joseph Bonaparte as King; this he had publicly burnt amid scenes of the greatest enthusiasm.

The Spanish regiments stationed in Minorca clamoured rowdily to be taken to the Peninsula to fight the enemy; their passage was paid by the Mahon authorities, to restore peace to the town. In their place came a great many refugees, mainly from Catalonia, who were lucky to have escaped the horrors of the French invasion. The town of Mahon had to be expanded to house these refugees, the majority of whom were fairly well off; among them was the future King Louis Philippe of France. This invasion brought together

Britain, Portugal and Spain as allies and the opening of the Peninsular campaigns of Sir Arthur Wellesley, later the Duke of Wellington. No British troops set foot again on Minorca but the Royal Navy returned to its base in Mahon harbour, and remained the principal protection of the Balearics against a possible French attack.

Lord Collingwood, who had been second-in-command to Nelson at Trafalgar and was now in command of the British Mediterranean fleet, came to Mahon in the autumn of 1809. Here his job was to blockade Toulon. Although only 61, he had been exhausted by a lifetime at sea and was already suffering from an internal complaint which was shortly to kill him. In the previous year he had begged the Admiralty to relieve him of his command, but they had replied in effect that they just could not do without him.

From Mahon he sailed to his last victory over the French, the destruction of a convoy and its escort of warships belonging to the Toulon squadron. He much regretted that only a part of the French fleet had emerged from its harbour. He returned to what is now called 'The Admiral's House' on the road between Mahon and Villa Carlos and took to his bed, because of the steadily increasing pain, yet from here he continued to deal with the great pressure of business. By February 1810, he could bear it no longer and sent in his resignation to the Lords of the Admiralty. On 3rd March, he went on board his flagship, *Ville de Paris*, to return home. It took the warship nearly three days to get clear of the harbour and on the following morning, 7th March, he died.

At the very beginning of the following year, Rear-Admiral Tom Fremantle, who had in the previous October hoisted his flag on the *Ville de Paris*, previously the flagship of Lord St. Vincent and Sir William Cornwallis as well as of Collingwood, was writing from Mahon to his brother: 'my great anxiety now is about this place, where there are eight good Spanish Ships of the line . . ., considering that in the course of a few Months the whole of Catalonia will probably be in the hands of the Enemy. I see with what facility they can, whilst our fleet are at Sea, take this Island by a coup de Main and turn all this force against us, there are not more than 600 Spanish troops here and melancholy to say one half of these are French Men who have been made prisoners, and now serving in the Walloons [Walloon Guards].'

He later reported that 'the very distressed state of the Spanish Marine in this port has rendered it necessary for the Commodore to expose for sale some part of the stores deposited in the Arsenal, to relieve their immediate wants, as well as to victual their Seamen and Marines.' Fremantle took this opportunity of purchasing cheaply some very fine timber to help the Spanish Commodore and, no doubt, to repair his own ships as well. He also had the satisfaction of seeing the arrival of Spanish army reinforcements as a result of his reports.

Minorca was never attacked during these years of war with France. This was perhaps just as well. The islanders are as brave as any other people anywhere, but they have always regarded freedom from military service as one of their rights, even at a time of national emergency, as in 1810 when all able-bodied men were needed to repel the French. The idea of serving, and perhaps dying, away from Minorca was too much for the Minorcans and riots broke out. Even the Bishop of Minorca sympathized with these insurgents, who rioted and destroyed many of the archives of Mahon, Alayor and Villa Carlos. Forceful measures were taken, the ringleader hanged and heavy fines imposed on the municipalities of Mahon and Alayor.

In 1820, when the draft was introduced again because of uprisings in Spain's South American colonies, there was no difficulty in filling the naval quota required, but the army quota was not so easily made up, in spite of the fact that the sons of rich families were allowed to pay someone else to take their place. The best way, however, of avoiding active service was to get married and in that year, called 'The Marriage Year', there was an unprecedented number of weddings.

The 1830s saw much emigration. Many young people went abroad to escape the poverty and hunger which were then widespread in Minorca. The majority were attracted by Algiers which, conquered by the French in 1830, seemed to offer considerable opportunities close at hand. Others went to South America, settling mainly in Argentina and Uruguay on both sides of the River Plate.

Minorca has been on excellent terms since early in the nineteenth century with the United States of America, whose navy used the Isla Plana in Mahon harbour as a training station, especially between 1825 and 1830; they also established a hospital there. With the opening of the U.S. Naval College at Annapolis, Mahon was far less frequently visited by the Americans, but the mutual warmth continued, partly because the first naval officer in the U.S. Navy ever to attain the rank of admiral had strong associations with the island. David Glasgow Farragut's father, of pure-bred Minorcan stock, claimed descent from a warrior who had served with distinction in James the Conqueror's conquest of Majorca and Valencia; he himself had left Minorca during the British occupation and settled in East Tennessee, where he married an American girl. His son David was born in 1801 and became a midshipman: at the age of fourteen he was in *U.S.S. Independence* when it was sent against the Algerian pirates. The American squadron spent the next two or three years in the Mediterranean and Farragut was in Mahon both in 1816 and 1817, although his journal at that time betrayed little interest in the island or its association with his family.

David Farragut gained great naval distinction during the American Civil War when serving on the Northern side. He commanded the Federal squadron in the Gulf of Mexico and along the lower reaches of the Mississipi where his blockade prevented the hard-pressed Southern States from receiving much needed help from Confederate areas to the west. His 'surest claim to glory', according to Captain Mahan, the distinguished American naval historian, was the battle of Mobile, in which he fought the Confederate *Tennessee*, an ironclad, and won. He was promoted vice-admiral in December 1864 and admiral eighteen months later, at the end of the 'war between the States'. He was then appointed to command the European squadron and in December 1867 dropped anchor in Mahon harbour.

On the day after Christmas, Farragut paid a visit to Ciudadela. Everywhere en route the welcome was enormous. He was met by the mayor of the town and driven in a handsome barouche to the residence, close to the cathedral, of Señor Don Gabriel Squella, which had been placed at his disposal—but he had to walk the last few yards as his carriage could not get through the enthusiastic crowds. An evening reception was followed next morning by a visit to places of interest, ending in the cathedral, 'in which he had scarcely been seated', recorded his secretary, 'before it was literally

packed in every part by people, their hundreds of eyes being riveted upon the pleasant countenance of the unappalled admiral ...'
It was Farragut's last visit to Minorca.

The labour situation on the island, which had forced many to emigrate during the 1830s, improved considerably during the next decade as a result of the decision to erect the great fortress of La Mola on the granite headland on the north-east side of the entrance to Mahon harbour. Not only were many Minorcans employed on this work but labourers also came from Ibiza, a number of whom acquired houses in Villa Carlos. The introduction, however, of steam marked the end of the harbour's importance; it was used less and less. Today only a few boats call. The garrison was accordingly withdrawn and the fortifications of La Mola abandoned.

Nevertheless, the unemployment problem was further improved in the 1850s by Don Jeronimo Cabrisas y Caymaris, a native of Ciudadela. Cabrisas, a shoemaker by training, had as a young man emigrated to Cuba where he had met with the *boniato* or sweet potato. This he successfully propagated on Minorca and then returned to the Caribbean to make his fortune. When he finally came back to Minorca he established in Ciudadela the shoemaking industry which has since spread to other centres and is now one of the most important on the island.

The rest of the nineteenth century was quieter on the island than in most of the Peninsula. Queen Isabel II visited Minorca as well as Majorca in 1860, going both to Mahon and Ciudadela. A growing number of political parties, supported by a flourishing political press, continued to reflect to some extent the traditional rivalries between the various local centres. Gas and electricity were introduced just before the turn of the century.

And so to the Spanish Civil War of 1936–39, which even in these remote islands saw political rivalries and ideologies flare into bloodshed, suffering and destruction. Ibiza and Majorca were held by the Nationalists, except, in the case of Ibiza, for a brief Republican interlude. In Minorca, the army commander, General Bosch, proclaimed the Nationalist cause, but was overpowered by the Republicans who were to maintain control throughout the conflict until almost the very end, although, especially in Ciudadela, there were a number who favoured the Nationalists. The island was not invaded during the War, probably because of the extensive coastal artillery defences, but was subjected to some bombardment from the Nationalist air force and their Italian allies, based on Majorca. Wheat was plentiful but there was a great shortage of such items as petrol, coffee, rice and sugar, as the island was heavily blockaded. Extreme left Republican elements executed some Nationalist sympathizers early on and damaged the several churches, both inside and out, in Mahon and Ciudadela, but for the most part an uneasy calm prevailed. The Civil War is not today a subject for general discussion, even though well over 30 years have passed since its conclusion.

The war was declared officially at an end on 1st April, 1939, but the surrender of Minorca to the Nationalists took place some weeks earlier under British auspices. *The Times* reported that, on 8th February, H.M.S. *Devonshire* had taken an emissary on behalf of General Franco to negotiate the occupation of the island. The discussions took place on board the British cruiser. On the following day, Nationalist troops were allowed to land with slight resistance only, and H.M.S. *Devonshire* left with 450 Minorcan refugees. 'The British diplomatic intervention in Minorca was successful yesterday,' said a *Times* leader on the 10th February, 'and a well-fortified island, that would have otherwise bravely, but in the end uselessly, have resisted transfer, has been peacefully and reasonably made over to the master of the greater part of Spain.'

⚜ 19 ⚜

Mahon

The approach to Mahon from the new airport, which lies to its south-west, does nothing to prepare the visitor for the fact that this little town with a population of 20,000, the largest community on the island, is a seaport. The stunted olive trees, meagre grass and drystone walls on each side of the dusty road suddenly give way to the new industrial estate, spread out beside the main Mahon— Ciudadela road. Turning east, the way towards the centre of Mahon is down the Avenida José Maria Quadrado, named after Minorca's distinguished historian, round the great Plaza Explanada, up the Calle Hannover and so in a few minutes to the Plaza Generalissimo Franco. Here on the busy thoroughfare stands the great church of St. Mary and the Mayor's office, with the Plaza de la Conquista close by. Through an arch at the far side of the Plaza the waters of the harbour come suddenly into view.

Mahon stands at the far south-west corner of the finest island harbour in the Mediterranean. The harbour itself stretches some three miles inland from Fort St. Philip at its mouth. Mahon is a white hilly town with narrow one-way streets traversing the slopes until, on the west side, the land merges into the island's central plateau. Below, at water level, there is just room for a road and a line of cottages and warehouses to nestle into the low cliffs besides the ample quays. Most of the town is about 80 feet higher and a broad avenue, the Abundancia, leads up from the quay where the passenger boats berth to the Plaza España. To the west of this lies the eighteenth-century town.

The streets are terraced with houses two and three storeys high. These are regularly whitewashed and have green or brown shutters; the gently sloping roofs are covered with reddish-brown tiles. Inside and out, the houses are spotlessly clean. Dust and rubbish is at once cleared away by proud housewives or their maids, even in the hottest summer weather, which can be as intense here as anywhere else in the Mediterranean.

It is possible that the English visitor will find something vaguely familiar about the design of these houses. The doorsteps, and particularly the sash-cord windows, give the clues; these houses were built during the British occupation of the eighteenth century and have been maintained in this style ever since. Only the sash-cords have given way to clips which fit into rungs down the side of the window frame and do not need constant renewal. J. E. Crawford Flitch, writing about Mahon in *Mediterranean Moods*, said that 'The houses were clearly built by a race that had not yet learned to fear the rigour of the Mediterranean sun. Moors and Spaniards, who built to exclude rather than to admit the light, space their windows economically in a generous extension of wall. In Mahon, they are painted largely and boldly, in rows of two and three, fitted with sashes and divided by laths of white-painted wood with six square panes—just as they are in the Hackney Road. The balcony—that one solace of women in southern lands—is almost as little known as in Devonport or Falmouth. The Church of Santa Maria, it is true, has a proper Mediterranean quality—the imposing simplicity which comes from sheer unrelieved expanse of wall; but its façade is made ridiculous by the intrusion of four sash windows, which give it something of the air of an eighteenth century meeting-house.'

Sir John Carr, one of the earliest travel-book writers, who was here in 1811, some years after the island's restoration to Spain, cheerfully noted the familiar touch: 'Sashed windows, the construction of their doors, steps to ascend them, knockers and scrapers, signs to the public houses.' Only the signs to the public houses have now been taken down. In any case, Mahon then as now was an exceptionally sober place. In those days, there was no proper water supply and each house relied upon its own cistern, into which several live eels were introduced to keep the water purified. If this did not work, an armful of the green tops of myrtle was thrown into the water. Only if both methods failed was the cistern actually cleaned out.

Towards the end of the last century the Archduke Louis Salvator on a visit to Minorca from Majorca, where he spent much of his life, was intrigued by the large street paving stones he discovered here and there, made of a stone not known on the island. With his usual initiative, he turned them over to find that they were British gravestones which had been sent out from England for deceased officers and soldiers. In the absence of a consul or War Graves Commission, these stone slabs had been collected from the un-attended graveyards and used to pave Mahon's streets.

Mahon may originally have been a Carthaginian settlement, but its real foundations were laid in Roman times. Later, both the Vandals in the fifth century and the Vikings in the ninth may have done much damage. At the time of the Reconquest a fort stood here, a place in which those living nearby could take shelter. There was a village of sorts around what is now the Plaza Generalissimo Franco and the streets now known as Isabel II, San Rocco and Iglesia, intersected by Buen Aire; it was around this area that Alfonso III in 1287 ordered walls to be erected. He also ordered the construction of a royal palace where the military governor's headquarters now stands.

By 1301 the local authorities had carried out most of Alfonso's building instructions and the outstanding work continued at a leisurely pace. In 1363 it was realized that the massively-built walls had been extended further than necessary. The pulling down of the unnecessary parts which followed was as unhurried as their construction had been. The whole defensive system later became largely obsolete with the construction of Fort St. Philip in the seventeenth century.

Today all that remains of the mediaeval walls is the great gateway and tower in the Plaza Bastion. Mahon began to expand in the seventeenth century and by the time the British arrived early in the eighteenth, there were 500 families. The British encouraged trade from which the local population benefited enormously and much of the inner part of Mahon was built at this time.

Of the fort or castle, the little that still existed disappeared under the stuccoed neo-classical Casa Mercadel which stands in the Plaza de la Conquista. Originally the home of a noble family, it now houses the Museo Provincial de Bellas Artes de Mahon. This eighteenth-century *palacio* bears the date '16 June 1761' on the entrance arch but much of the interior is very much older, dating back to mediaeval times. This fine mansion is built on one of the highest parts of the town; the centre of the settlement which Mago encountered when he arrived in 205 B.C. may have been here.

The Museo de Bellas Artes de Mahon is well laid-out and its contents cover the whole of Minorca's history. The ground floor is devoted to collections ranging from the *talayot* culture to Carthaginian, Iberian, Greek and Roman finds. Most, but not all, of these are ceramic but other items of note include an elegantly wrought breastplate, described as Celtic, and a fine collection of coins. A large-scale map shows the whereabouts of the island's principal prehistoric monuments. In addition there is the mosaic pavement which was discovered on the Isla del Rey in the middle of the harbour near the end of the nineteenth century. There is also a small but interesting display of Aztec and Mayan objects.

Most of the first floor is occupied by the fine public library which is much in use. In the first-floor rooms overlooking the square is a small collection of paintings, including one of George III in early middle age, and of Charlotte, his Queen, by an unknown hand. There are also portraits of the Conde de Cifuentes attributed to Pascual Calbo and of Dr. Orfila by Esquivel. Finally, in this section, there is the room devoted to the Port of Mahon which includes maps, models of ships, and views of the harbour, including fine examples of the landscapes of Juan Font. There is also a small but fine collection of eighteenth-century books, manuscripts, cartoons and prints, dating from the British occupation of Minorca, collected by Mr. Jim Maps, an American long resident on the island.

In the middle of the Plaza de la Conquista outside stands the bold, full-length statue of the young Alfonso III, an expression of youthful arrogance on his face as he looks imperiously over the island he has conquered. The name of the donor, Dr. Francisco Franco y Bahemonde (General Franco) is on the west side of the great granite plinth.

The tall golden church of St. Mary, the principal church in Mahon, with its high altar at the north instead of the more usual east end, stands on the west side of the square. Its construction was originally started in 1287, immediately after the Reconquest; then it was completely rebuilt between 1748 and 1772. Some have suggested that this reconstruction was intended as a gesture of defiance against the Protestant British, financed perhaps by the expanding trade which the British encouraged.

St. Mary's has a severe Baroque exterior and an undistinguished octagonal belfry, but inside there is much of interest. The nave, without aisles, has a Gothic ceiling. Gothic side-chapels stand within the interior buttresses which support the outer walls: at one time there were evidently galleries above these chapels, but the way through the buttress walls has been blocked in. At the north end is a sumptuous Baroque marble altar, which rises to the ceiling, flanked by Solomonic pillars and with much elaborate stonework around the doorway to the right of the altar. The apse had several chapels but they were rendered completely useless by the size of the altar. The elevated gallery above the south entrance, supported by the shallow arch, common in Balearic Baroque, is now occupied by a vast Austrian organ. Two of the French governors who ruled Minorca between 1756 and 1763 are commemorated in St. Mary's and their names—the Comte de Lannion and the Marquis de Fremeur—are on tablets let into the walls of the south entrance of the church, one on each side.

Immediately to the north of the church of St. Mary on the Plaza Generalissimo Franco is the Ayuntamiento or Town Hall. It is an elaborately decorated building in the Neo-classical manner, dating from 1613, but its considerable charm is somewhat spoiled by being so closely hemmed in by other buildings. In the entrance hall is the British coat-of-arms taken from Fort St. Philip. There are also portraits of former governors and notabilities, including Sir Richard Kane, who presented the building with a clock.

A feeling of restraint and dignity fills the long, brooding Calle de Isabel II with its tall patrician houses at the end nearest to the Ayuntamiento. They back on to the low cliffs which overlook the harbour. Below are the quays and warehouses. There are no gardens facing the water; but some houses contrive to have a tiny space inside, lit by a skylight, in which a few green plants flourish. The front part of the ground floor facing the street is sometimes used as offices, but the first floor, the *piso principal*, usually contains formal reception rooms and in at least one case a state bedroom. There are excellent English eighteenth-century Georgian chairs and tables, made in Minorca by skilful Minorcan craftsmen who faultlessly copied the pattern books of English furniture designers of the period such as Chippendale and Sheraton; their work today is highly prized.

Halfway down the Calle Isabel II is the headquarters of the military governor, after which the street widens a little; the houses here are less distinguished. The military governor's building, consisting of two storeys and standing white and sparkling above its spacious courtyard, is faintly reminiscent of a British colonial governor's residence with its wide, deep-shaded balconies. It was in fact built by the British during the eighteenth century, but was then of only one storey. On its walls are prints of the history of Mahon, including several connected with the British occupation and their subsequent departure.

The church of St. Francis (San Francisco) at the far end of the Calle Isabel II is beautiful. The pale golden stone of the plain Baroque facade, the simple yet elegant decoration of the parapet and belfry, and the round Romanesque doorway into the church are an unusual combination. The church is not built with its altar at the east end, but the other way round, because of the demands of the site. To the north, some way below, lie the peaceful waters of the harbour. The great nave, without aisles, stands higher than the neighbouring square four-storied cloister buildings which enclose an open courtyard with a well in the centre. This once contained the dormitories of the friars. It is now used as an orphanage and is not normally open to the public.

The church was built sometime after Mahon had been destroyed in 1535 by Kheir-ed-Din Barbarossa, during the seventeenth and eighteenth centuries. The date 1738 in one of the side-chapels may indicate that the nave had been completed by then. The apse, in the Baroque manner, bears the date 1791. Its structure reveals, as is also the case in Majorca, how loyal the Balearic builders were to the Gothic style during the Baroque period. The Romanesque doorway is exceptionally intriguing: this style was largely out of fashion in western Europe when the Reconquest of Majorca took place in 1230, and there is hardly any architecture in the Romanesque manner to be found on that island. Alfonso III's seizure of Minorca took place nearly 60 years later. Almost certainly this doorway was an experiment by the architect of St. Francis', dating from the time when the church was built, and a very successful one.

The church has an ogival roof in six sections with curious

bas-relief columns at the side under classical capitals: there are five side-chapels down each side. The altar is supported by heavy Solomonic pillars—gold on dark brown—and flanked on each side by a great panel depicting Biblical scenes in black and grey—an imaginative detail.

The most exciting feature of the church, however, is the large chapel dedicated to the Immaculate Conception which is entered by the middle side-chapel on the north. This chapel is octagonal in shape, surmounted by a dome on top of which is an octagonal lantern. Inside, the dome rests on heavy Solomonic pillars, in the grooves of which climb the stems of flowering plants. Between the pillars are eight small chapels. The overall decoration is reminiscent of the principal side-chapel, dedicated to St. Nicholas of Tolentino, of Neustra Señora del Socorro in Palma, which was the work of Francisco Herrera. Both show intertwining vegetation, the rose with the vine, together with decorations which might be classified as 'Churrigueresque', that is the Spanish Baroque style in its most fantastic form.

It is not known whether or not Francisco Herrera—who is not to be confused with Juan de Herrera, the disciple of Michaelangelo and leader of the classical movement in Spain—was responsible for this lovely chapel in the church of St. Francis; we do know that after training in Rome, he came in 1680 to work in Minorca for ten years before journeying to Majorca, where he worked on the west front of St. Francis in Palma and the chapel in Nuestra Señora del Socorro. Perhaps some architectural detective may eventually confirm a connection between Francisco Herrera and the church of St. Francis in Mahon. It was badly damaged during the Spanish Civil War of 1936–39 but has since been well restored.

The third great church is very much less interesting than St. Mary's or St. Francis'. This is the Carmen church on the Plaza del Carmen, once a Carmelite convent; it was built in 1751. It stands almost as high to the east of the Plaza d'España as St. Mary's does to the west. Its Baroque west front is exceptionally plain and severe, characteristics which are repeated in its light and spacious interior. There is a nave and two aisles in which the side-chapels are sited. The largest chapel is formed from part of the apse behind the altar, the rest of the apse being devoted to office accommodation. Like other churches, the Carmen suffered from vandalism during the

Spanish Civil War, but has since been restored. The market which is permanently established in the cloisters of the convent is covered, and the interior garden merely the repository for rubbish. Many of the booths display for sale the delicious Mahon cheese and, on occasion, bottles of Mahon gin, distilled locally according to a formula introduced by the British navy in the eighteenth century; its manufacture is an important local industry.

In John Armstrong's day, the Carmelite convent was a little way out of town: today, because of the spread of the town, it is almost central. He reported that on the opening up of the foundations to begin the new church, a great many Roman coins, lamps, urns and other relics were discovered. Some contemporaries of his were of the opinion that this might have been the old Roman cemetery. Many more relics may in due course be discovered, should it ever become practical to explore what is buried in this area.

References to an English past are frequent in Mahon; even the occasional English word has managed to survive here, inevitably with a slight change. Thus 'marbles' become '*mervels*', 'pilchards' '*pinxas*', 'bow-window' '*boinder*', and so forth. The only place name in Mahon which recalls the English occupation is the Calle Hannover, a pleasant street in the centre of the town, whose surrounding buildings were built when the English influence was largely over. There was a notable absence of balconies on the houses erected when the Hanoverian kings reigned over Minorca. Subsequently, as if to compensate for lack of quantity by quality, a number of beautiful first-floor glass enclosed balconies have been added to houses in this area, jutting out over the streets.

Moving westwards, the Calle Hannover becomes the tree-lined Paseo Dr. Orfila. Close by, in the Calle Conde de Cifuentes, its rear facing on to the Plaza Explanada, is the Ateneo, a distinguished centre of learning and teaching, with valuable natural history collections, especially of sea weed, for which it is known far beyond Mahon. It has a good library, publishes the results of its members' researches, and provides an agreeable meeting place for Mahon's intelligentsia: concerts and lectures are included in its activities.

ᨩ 20 ᨦ

South-east Minorca

Many famous English seamen visited Mahon during the eighteenth and early nineteenth centuries. One of them was the future Admiral Lord Rodney, whose crowning achievement was to be his victory over the French off Dominica in 1782, which perhaps compensated for the British loss of Fort St. Philip in the same year. Rodney was however only seventeen when the *Dreadnought*, in which he was then serving, came to anchor in Mahon harbour for some seven weeks in 1735.

The young officer would have seen several things which are unchanged or only slightly altered today. There was the naval hospital, built in 1711 on the instructions of Admiral Sir John Jennings, then British commander-in-chief in the Mediterranean, on the Isla del Rey, or King's Island, halfway along the length of the harbour. Alfonso III had disembarked here in 1287 when he came to seize Minorca from the Moors; to the British the island was known generally as 'Bloody Island'. According to Grasset de St. Sauveur, the British hospital was later altered or added to during the first Spanish occupation in 1773–76, and was functioning until fairly recently. The French made use of its facilities during their brief occupation and the American navy employed it as a training centre in the 1820s. In John Armstrong's day an oyster cove existed on the south shore facing the hospital, and today rafts float nearby from which long chains are suspended to encourage the growth of excellent mussels.

Rodney would also have been able to see the collection of incredibly run-down and battered hulks, once part of the Spanish fleet. They had been captured in 1718 in the battle off Cape Passaro, Sicily, by a British fleet under the command of Sir George Byng. Seventeen years later, a decision about their disposal was still

177

awaited. Sir George Byng later became Lord Torrington and it was his younger son, the Hon. John Byng, who was executed at Portsmouth in 1757 for his supposed failure against the French navy off Minorca. Of this incident Voltaire had Candide remark that 'in this country [England] it is thought well to kill an admiral from time to time to encourage the others.'

Rodney was likely to have known Fort St. Philip, of which little is to be seen today, as most of it was inexplicably razed to the ground by the Spanish authorities in 1807, a year before the French invasion of the Peninsula. The area is controlled by the military and is normally out of bounds but it is still possible to visit the ruins of the Marlborough Redoubt and from there to see what little is left of the fort on the far side of St. Stephen's cove. The Redoubt can be reached by turning right to the fort off the San Luis–Villa Carlos road via Trebaluger and then turning right again down a rough track leading to the *barranco*, or ravine, which extends inland from St. Stephen's cove. Follow this until the cove itself is reached, and here, on the hillside, is seen what is left of the Marlborough Redoubt, once a formidable fortification. Its guns covered the approach to the fort from the east and south-east and its position made surprise well nigh impossible. As long as those in the Redoubt could be replenished with ammunition and provisions, it was a great thorn in the side of an attacker. The French were lucky to seize the 'shallop' which the British in the Redoubt used to keep in touch with the main defences across St. Stephen's Cove. In the final assault, the Redoubt was defended by a captain and 50 men only, but are said to have beaten off an attacking force of some 700 men commanded, according to one contemporary account, by a Prince of the Blood. Its strength is amply vindicated.

On the north side of the cove with its gently lapping water are a few stone huts and emplacements of Fort St. Philip. Originally the fort consisted of four bastions connected by curtain walls behind a deep ditch hewn out of the solid rock. Inside stood the Governor's house, barracks, guard-room and a chapel, and the whole rock was undermined with subterranean chambers and passageways, some of which are still used by the Spanish army today. Close to its outer walls further buildings grew up which were to restrict the defenders' field of fire in 1756. The deliberate destruction of the fort in 1807 was well carried out. Beyond the fort can be seen the granite headland of La Mola on the far side of the harbour entrance. It is worth climbing to the top of the Redoubt, which can easily be reached, in order to enjoy the views of the island and out to sea, including that to the south, where the British defenders first saw Byng's fleet sail into sight in 1756.

The cliffside of the *barranco* beyond St. Stephen's cove has been hollowed out into caves which have been made into habitations with stuccoed façades to give them the appearance of houses. 200 years ago, fruit trees and vegetables grew here in sufficient profusion to supply Mahon and the surrounding villages. Today it provides a delightful, cool summer retreat by the water while Mahon is enveloped in heat. On the green slopes rising from the sea along the coast to the south of the Marlborough Redoubt are several defence towers of various dates. An enjoyable walk, high above the Mediterranean, can be had here.

Rodney's naval career never brought him back to Mahon and so he would not, for example, have known Georgetown, built during the second British occupation in the 1770s both as a garrison and as a residential town. Today known as Villa Carlos, it has expanded in the direction of the Trepucó *talayot* and *taula*. Many villas have been built and an English colony has grown up here, one reason for this being the excellent roads to Mahon and San Luis, and from there to several coastal resorts in the south-east corner of Minorca.

In the heart of Villa Carlos is the vast, square British parade ground and, around it, the unexpectedly elegant-looking British barracks. The parade ground is no longer used as such. A road now runs through the centre and trees have been planted in several parts of it. Troops, however, still occupy the barracks, one of which is named after the Duc de Crillon. The former British presence here is acknowledged by a road named Stewart, presumably referring to the Stuart dynasty which twice, during the first half of the eighteenth century, failed to regain the English throne from the House of Hanover, whose realm included Minorca. On festival days, local girls are said on occasion to wear what is recognizably a tartan kilt and to dance a variation of a highland fling. In the harbour, nearer to the north than the south side and opposite Villa Carlos, is the Isla Plana which used to be the Quarantine Island until it was superseded; it was used for a time by the United States navy in the nineteenth century.

Pleasant corners of the town can be explored, especially near the harbour where the British influence is more pronounced. There are also some good civic buildings, including the town hall. Admiral Collingwood's house, now a small but well-planned hotel, is not in the centre of Villa Carlos, but along the road towards Mahon. It has a pleasant classical façade and in the public rooms inside are some excellent prints of the harbour during the eighteenth century, and of British and Spanish uniforms. The outside walls are painted a rich plum red, not a colour usually associated with the Balearics, where white is almost universal. One Spanish writer commenting on this unusual hue, associates it with the British and therefore regards it as a corruption of local purity. It has however been used elsewhere on the island with considerable effect, and the best hotel in Mahon has long been painted this colour.

Another house in the same general style as the Admiral's House is San Antoni, a fine building in the classical manner. It stands at the top of the slope above the north side of the harbour, facing across to the Cala Figuera on the south side; in Armstrong's time this was called the English Cove, because it was the British navy's watering place.

Otherwise known as Golden Farm, San Antoni has two storeys, the lower of which is painted white and the upper a rich reddish-terracotta. A deep-set balcony with three arches stands over the main entrance and above this is an elegant little pediment on which classical figures airily recline. Lord Nelson, according to local tradition, stayed here for two or three days during his brief visit to Minorca in October 1799. The view of the harbour and of Mahon beyond is one of the finest on the island. An ornamental garden has been built below the terrace where several fine palm trees flourish. Lower still is ploughland, woods and villas by the water's edge. Delightful airy spaciousness surrounds this graceful house on all sides.

The rough road along the north side of the harbour moves inland from the naval base before swinging round to San Antoni after passing the track up to Cala Mezquida. Beyond San Antoni, the road leading on to La Mola is open and exposed. On the far side of the road, away from the harbour's waters, stands a cross bearing the date of 2nd August 1936 which commemorates the Nationalists executed here by their Republican enemies early in the Civil War. No entrance is permitted to the gaunt, neglected barracks of La Mola. Round about, the land, like sand blown by the wind, has been moulded into small curiously-shaped hills, the haunt of partridges and other birds.

In the harbour below lies the largest of its several islands. Here is the *lazareto* or quarantine station. This group of buildings was constructed on the orders of the Royal Minister, Count Floridablanca, during the first Spanish occupation of Minorca. Turning back towards Mahon, a little graveyard may be noticed down by the water's edge, facing across to the Isla del Rey. This is the English cemetery, a calm and peaceful place. Only a few tombs stand within the whitewashed walls which keep it separate from the rough heathland surrounding it.

Along the east shore up to the Isla del Colom (or in Catalan, Illa d'en Colom), the largest island off the east coast of Minorca, are some fine beaches and the beginnings of several *urbanizacion* or building developments, out of which holiday resorts will grow. One of the first is at the Cala Mezquida with its massive old fort on the rocks above the beach. It was here that part of the Franco–Spanish army under the Duc de Crillon landed in August 1781, the rest coming ashore at Cala d'Alcaufar, south of Mahon harbour. Es Grau is another area where villas are springing up. It stands to the east of a narrow inlet into a large inland lake of salt water, as implied by its name, S'Albufera ('salt lagoon'). Armstrong called it the *Buferas* and remarked on the excellent fish that teemed in its waters and the great variety of wildfowl that sheltered here in winter. Shrubbery grows over the low surrounding hills through which the rich terracotta earth gleams in patches above the sandy beaches. The Isla del Colom is due north of Es Grau; its name derives from the vast number of wild pigeons which once bred in its rocky cliffs. This wild islet is said to contain the site of an early Christian church.

Two other beaches in this area deserve to be mentioned, both of them lying between the Isla del Colom and Fornells. The long, narrow peaceful inlet of Addaia allowed sufficient room for the British transport ships to manoeuvre in order to land their troops here in 1798. Over 50 years earlier, Armstrong had found this the most exquisite place on the whole island, with its low tree-clad protective hills encircling the tiny port. He wrote much about its fruit and vegetable gardens, its scenery and climate. 'You will say I wrote this in a romantick Humour: I confess it freely; and I shall ever think of *Adaia*, and of the company I enjoyed at that charming little Retirement, with the utmost Complacency and Satisfaction.' Today a spit of land which points north-east towards the rocks at the entrance to the inlet is being developed for the building of villas.

Arenal d'en Castell lies to the north-west of Addaia. Its wide, gently sweeping sandy bay, nearly two miles in length, is bounded by rocky promontories jutting out into the sea. Pine trees grow on the inland slopes behind it. Here, also, *urbanizacion* is in hand.

Many of the older developments are to be found in the south-east corner of the island, along the stretch of coastline running west from S'Algar to Cala'n Porter. Most of these mushrooming resorts are reached through San Luis and traffic has grown sufficiently here for a by-pass round the village to be necessary. San Luis was founded during the French occupation of 1756–63 in the reign of Louis XV. The long main street is flanked on both sides by low, whitewashed terraced houses. Streets run parallel on both sides, crossed at right angles by other streets. Behind them are market gardens with farmlands beyond.

The whitewashed Neo-classical church of San Luis, small and graceful and dedicated to the memory of St. Louis, King of France, stands centrally in the main street. Across the road facing the west façade is a small traffic-free square, its edges marked out by ever-green trees and surrounded on three sides by houses; there are stone seats with a small, graceful obelisk at the far end. The houses often have the Minorcan equivalent of sash windows already noticed in Mahon, in spite of San Luis's foundation being French. Inside the church are four small chapels on each side of the single nave whose well-proportioned height is supported by outside buttresses resting on top of the side-chapels. There is a small gallery over the west entrance. The barrel-vaulted ceiling with ogival treatment looks down on a church empty of any other decoration, except that the walls have been painted to resemble marble which is in no way offensive. The coat of arms of a cardinal can be seen on the wall inside the west entrance, and on the west front is an inscription bearing the date 1761; the coat of arms of Louis XV of France, of the Comte de Lannion, the most successful of the French governors, and of Antoine de Causan, the energetic administrator of the island under the French crown, are also displayed here. Only the bell-tower at the church's north-east corner provides a flavour of a much older past, a style reminiscent of a minaret of the Moorish period; otherwise the eighteenth century is triumphant.

The well-metalled roads move off between drystone walls, sometimes whitewashed along the top, to S'Algar, Cala Binian-colla, Cala de Binibeca, Cala de Binissafuller, Cala de Biniparraitx and other coastal resorts. The names are Moorish but the architec-ture of the newly-sprouting villas is on the whole pleasantly unpretentious with no traces of Islam except for the ever popular palm tree, a favourite decorative feature, as seen at S'Algar. The palm tree standing near the entrance to a house is a symbol of wel-come. One of the more remarkable developments is at Binibeca. Here, an extensive group of buildings has been erected above the little harbour, partially imitating fishermens' houses but providing excellent homes or holiday villas in an atmosphere both intimate yet impersonal. Alleyways run apparently at random through the complex, leading into little squares and continuing at right angles down smaller passageways. Some apartments are at ground level, others up stairways; some face inwards but most have a view of the sea. Here is obviously a design which will be adopted elsewhere.

At Cala Biniancolla, opposite the Isla del Aire, the houses are less sophisticated and stand on the rocky foreshore at the edge of the inlet. Even deeper is the inlet of Binidali; the limestone cliffs to the west of the entrance are pitted and hollowed by the sea and its villas for the most part are close to the sandy beach further inland where the shelter is greater.

West of the new airport along this coast with its low cliffs and little coves are the beginnings of further developments. Narrow tracks at present serving isolated farms will one day be found to be quite inadequate for the resultant *urbanizacion*, and so they will be widened and straightened and their surface metalled. Conse-quently the tempo for the building of new villas will be accelerated and branches of the metalled road will be extended to serve fresh developments—this process has already taken place at many established resorts. A continuous coastal road from S'Algar to Cala'n Porter does not yet exist, but it is not perhaps completely out of the question sometime during the 1980s.

The little sandy bay at the back of the inlet of Cala'n Porter has attracted a great concourse of villas and bungalows, neatly laid out wherever a foothold has been available on the rocky surface of the gently sloping land above the jagged cliffs. This is essentially a place for sea and sunbathing only. Trees do not grow readily here, and it is unlikely than many greater suntraps can be found anywhere in Minorca or even the Balearics.

⚝ 21 ⚝

Between Mahon and Ciudadela

The well-metalled main road across the island is wide enough for vehicles to pass comfortably. Running westward from Mahon between stone walls, sometimes reinforced with thorn hedges, as far as Alayor it has almost the straightness of a Roman road. The country is hilly and here and there on the slopes stand white-washed green-shuttered stone houses, bearing the name of the owner or of the house above the entrance. The fields are mainly devoted to pasture and both cattle and sheep abound. Building along the road is beginning to increase and recently two cement factories have been erected.

As Alayor draws near, indications of another road running parallel on the ridge to the north, less than a kilometre away, can be seen. This is the original cross-island route built by Richard Kane when he first took up his appointment as Lieutenant Governor of Minorca in 1713. Although it is a dirt road, it is in excellent condition and is almost as wide as the main road of today. It is extremely straight and offers wonderful views of Monte Toro in the distance. Here and there are large south-facing villas standing in their own grounds. Kane's road continues independently as far as Mercadel, where the mass of Monte Toro forces it to join the modern road just before it reaches the central village of the island.

Between Kane's road and the modern road from Mahon to Fornells is hilly, wooded country. Sunny little fields lie in the valleys. Geologically, this is the heartland of the island's Devonian rock-formation, and there is a complete absence of prehistoric monuments here. The hamlets are tiny and the houses scattered. Trees provide more shade than in the rest of the island, and the sea seems remote and forgotten. A journey into an area virtually unknown to the tourist can be quickly made and should give much quiet pleasure.

White and terracotta Alayor with its windmills, rising 'high and airy', to quote Armstrong, away from the main road towards the north, looks more impressive from a distance than close at hand. It is undoubtedly a prosperous town, the third largest on the island, and growing in size as more people drift away from the land. The main industry here is the manufacture of men's shoes and slippers of excellent quality, as well as some fine women's shoes. There is also some agriculture, and the island's supplies of ice cream are refrigerated here. The two churches are dedicated to Santa Eulalia and San Diego (St. James), but they do not compare in interest and beauty with those of Ciudadela and Mahon. Santa Eulalia when we visited it was so dark that it was virtually impossible to see the interior. San Diego was completely gutted during the Civil War.

According to Armstrong, an excellent woodcarver worked here in the first half of the eighteenth century. He possessed the vision of an artist and created several altars and sculpted many figures of the highest order. An elderly female concierge thought she had heard of such work but said it had been destroyed in the Civil War, if not earlier. One of the churches was used by the English, said Armstrong, 'whenever it happens that a Man of War lies in the Harbour that has a Chaplain belonging to it.' Is it possible that Armstrong's publisher allowed a paragraph about Mahon to slip into the Alayor section of his book? Is it difficult to imagine even the most religiously fervent naval captain marching his crew eight miles in Mediterranean heat along a dusty road for matins and another eight miles back. Perhaps this physical toughness was normal before the age of the motorcar.

Armstrong reported in his day that many of the people in Alayor were 'conversable and obliging, when we have once got their language' and that provisions were plentiful. Grasset de St. Sauveur at the beginning of the nineteenth century was very much more critical. He grumbled about the dirty bed linen at the *Casa del Rey*, with which Armstrong had been quite content 60 years earlier, and about the poor food—bad cheese, onions, detestable wine and greyish bread. So few travellers stayed in Spanish inns in those days that the occasional traveller had to pay for the upkeep of the inn and the innkeeper—the fewer the customers, the greater the expense. St. Sauveur tells of a Spanish officer who was forced when travelling by himself to stay in an inn where a vast charge was made. Two years later the same officer with a detachment of troops passed through the same village and a meal was ordered for them all at the same inn. On receiving the bill, the officer offered only a few sous. In response to the innkeeper's indignant protests, the officer explained that he had payed for the meal he had just eaten two years previously. The innkeeper had eventually to give way.

The Alayor district is perhaps richer in prehistoric monuments than any other in Minorca, especially in the area off the good secondary road running south-east and then south towards Cala'n Porter. Two of the island's newest roads have been built nearby. One runs down to the new resort of San Jaime, and the other, branching off the Alayor—Mercadel road further on, leads to the village of San Cristobal and to the beaches and hotels of San Tomas, whose pale golden sands are among the most attractive on the island. San Cristobal is mainly of recent origin and is pleasantly unexceptional, situated in lovely hilly country. The roads climb and descend, often quite steeply, as, for example, along the first few hundred yards of the way to San Tomas. Apart from the very occasional cottage or distant farmhouse, the scenery is virtually empty of people, the only moving objects being birds of prey hovering over the fields.

One of the most attractive stretches of road on the whole island must be that from San Cristobal to Ferrerias. It swings steeply down from the village, then round and up between two walls of limestone, overgrown with shrubbery, and on through upland country. The height of the road is always changing and there is a profusion of trees, including several umbrella pines which stand by the roadside with a pretence of giving shade. There are bridges over streams which are only filled with water for a brief time in the spring; one of them stands at the entrance into Ferrerias. Equally attractive is the road from San Cristobal to Mercadel running through farmlands, twisting round hillsides and through valleys, and finally skirting the hill of Puig Mal, rising to some 675 feet, before Mercadel is reached.

The main Mahon—Ciudadela road itself becomes more interesting soon after leaving Alayor as Monte Toro comes into view. Hills and slopes extend on both sides, and green meadows come up close to the roadside. Stone walls, sometimes with whitewashed tops, or posts each joined to the next by lengths of white material follow the road as it sweeps through valleys and over the slopes beyond. It is a fast stretch of road and a favourite with the traffic police.

The centre of the island is Monte Toro at whose feet lies the large village of Mercadel, which is now growing in size. All the houses are as usual white, as are the one or two small factories. The approach to Monte Toro is from here. Standing halfway up the mountain, the scenery does not look as if it belongs to the sea-girt Balearics, but might be an extension of Alpine pastures—green fields, with stone walls dividing them into irregular shapes, in which black and white cattle graze, and an occasional stone thresh-ing-floor, completely circular and perfectly laid, so different to the stamped earth of the Majorcan threshing-floors. In the background are the ranges of green hills, partly covered with woods, which stand between Mercadel and Ferrerias and stretch on to the north-west in the direction of the coast. A stone quarry from which some of the island's best building stone, a greyish granite, is excavated can be seen in the side of the mountain.

Monte Toro, over 1,000 feet high, is crowned by a monastery. Outside an enormous plinth surmounted by a figure of Christ has been raised to commemorate those who fell in the Civil War. A road winds steeply upwards from the town to the top from where the views are exciting; over half of Minorca can be seen and identified.

The name of Monte Toro has usually been associated with a bull cult. Vuillier wrote in 1896: 'At the beginning of this century the greatest treasure of the monastery, then tenanted by Augustine monks, was a rude sculpture, representing a bull hewing out a statue of the Virgin with its horns. The name of the mountain was said to be derived from this miracle, but a more probable etymology is that Toro comes from the word Tor, meaning elevation.' Over 150 years earlier, John Armstrong had reached the same conclusion, adding that El Tor (the mountain) was Moorish, which it is. St. Sauveur was of the same opinion and thought it an ideal site for a castle.

Instead it has always been occupied by a monastery or convent. In 1969 the church was tended by hermits, sent there from the sanctuary on the Puig de Maria above Pollensa in Majorca. By

1973 they had departed and, an order of nuns being in residence, the whole monastic building, including the church, shone immaculately.

Some five miles to the north of Mercadel is the little fishing village of Fornells. It stands close to the sea on the west side of a vast inlet, approaching Mahon harbour in size. A fort became necessary just to the north of the village because this great sheet of water was being used in the seventeenth century as a shelter by corsairs. St. Sauveur mentions that another fort, much of which still stands today was built by the British on the islet on the east side to provide crossfire with the main fort opposite. This faced east towards the great bare headland of Fornells, high up on which a signal station was erected. He also says that the British built a hospital here.

Today little is left of the main fort which the British kept in good repair. St. Sauveur noted that they converted the little chapel into a tavern for the troops and John Armstrong wrote of the matter as if it needed some justification, revealing one unexpected duty, by present-day standards, of at least one eighteenth-century garrison commander. 'The Commanding Officers', he wrote, 'have of late converted the Chapel into a Cellar; and as the *Minorquins* were heretofore comforted from hence with *holy Sprinklings* and *Benedictions*, our Soldiers have their Hearts no less rejoiced by the *Wine* and *Strong-Waters* here retailed to them at *a very reasonable price* by their *Commandant*, who is the *Suttler of the Garrison*.'

Today there is no question of a military or naval function for Fornells. The village faces south-east into the bay, pushing out a long breakwater to protect the fishing boats in the harbour from the dangers of a north wind and a rising sea. The palm trees which stand vigorously along the quay are no more troubled by the winter storms than are the inhabitants. In spring, these trees serve as shelters for innumerable linnets. With the exception of the palm trees, there is something almost clinical about the whitewashed houses with green shutters and an occasional orange door, standing in terraced lines, without contrasts between one house and the next, and without gardens. But here, at the northern extremity of the island, the vegetation is sparse and a walk to the ruins of the fort and the seashore reveals little except rock, only partly covered with moss. For much of the winter this is soaked by blown spume from the waves as they beat against the shore.

Fornells, too, is growing. The newer houses stand along the road from Mercadel and sport heavy protection on the north side against bad weather. One or two restaurants exist in the village, and on the water's edge one or two cafés have been established on the approach roads to the village. The metalled open space by the harbour has been marked out into a great many parking lots, showing how very popular this resort is becoming with Minorcans and visitors alike. Just to the south of the great inlet is Cap des Port where traces of an early Christian basilica have been discovered.

The north coast with its headlands, bays and still unspoilt beaches, backed here and there by cliffs, is among the loveliest and wildest parts of the island. If this enchanted coastline were in Britain, the National Trust, conscious that about a third of its coastline has already been ruined beyond redemption, would be making every effort to acquire it in order to preserve it unspoilt for the nation. The Minorcans, on the other hand, backed by inter-national finance, are intent upon developing it for tourism. One such area is from the beach of Binimel-la north-eastwards to the Cap de Cavalleria, the island's most northerly point. A secondary road, marked on local maps as leading to the Cap de Cavalleria, sets off from Mercadel on the far side of the *torrente* bed in a north-westerly direction. The going is fair at first but deteriorates proportionately as the beauty of the countryside increases. It meanders between green pastures, hedgerows of privet and occa-sional brakes of timber, bounded by rolling, hilly country which is largely devoid of trees. Then, when there appears to be little point in going any further because of the state of the road, a fine wide highway suddenly presents itself, leading direct to the coast which is a kilometre away. Running close to the beach, it continues up and around the flank of the great foreland which dominates the Cap de Cavalleria beyond, and all of it is apparently due for development.

Ferrerias is the last village of any importance before the final stretch of road to Ciudadela. From Mercadel the road moves west across level country, then quickly begins to climb up into the steep surrounding wooded hills, but still dominated by Monte Toro to the east, although with the next bend in the road the mountain and its monastery have disappeared from view. This is the hilliest region of Minorca with summits ranging from between 600 and 900 feet. After maintaining height, the road begins to descend towards Ferrerias, the largest centre on the island after Alayor, built inside the bend formed by the meeting of the two roads from Mercadel and San Cristobal. Above these roads the hills rise steeply so that Ferrerias is tucked down into a hollow which is inclined to be airless. Its terraced houses climb up and down the hillside and nearly every other house, which ten years ago must surely have been for domestic use only, seems to be a shop. There is a simple, little Baroque church which is quite unremarkable. Ferrerias has not even the satisfaction of fine views, such as Mercadel enjoys of Monte Toro, but its quiet, engaging population thrives.

Just to the west of Ferrerias, a road turns south. It is broad and featureless, running between fertile fields and valleys and passing the occasional stretch of pinewood until it makes its way down towards the loveliest of blue waters beckoning from beyond a broad sandy bay surrounded by tall pine-covered cliffs. Santa Galdana has always been considered one of the balmiest, perhaps the most unspoilt, of bays along the south coast. There is even a brook which in spring trickles into the waters of the bay, its path marked by a profusion of greenery along the banks. One enormous hotel, almost cliff high, and two or three smaller ones, together with a number of holiday cottages, have grown up over a period of four years and the beauty of Santa Galdana is inevitably diminished and standardized.

Most excursions off the main east-west highway involve making a return journey, but distances in Minorca are very small and the main road is only ten minutes away from Santa Galdana. An unsigned lane turns off into the north and straggles towards the coast through higher ground, one branch ending at Santa Agueda, or Agatha, which can be seen from quite a distance. Vuillier wrote 'the most striking feature (of the view from the summit of Monte Toro) is the steep bare hill of Santa Agueda, which was one of the oldest military posts in the island. The Romans took advantage of this commanding position, and at a later date the Moors made it a stronghold, where they held out for a long time against the forces of Alfonso III. The fortress which still stood at the beginning of the century, is now a ruin, and what is left intact has been converted into a farm building.' The Moors did not, of course, hold out against Alfonso III, but sent envoys to meet him in order to negotiate terms. The views are indeed impressive but the remains of Roman and Moor are insignificant, and difficult to disentangle from each other. Below stretches the north coast at its wildest with only one or two small sandy beaches.

The road to Ciudadela continues over and down the side of a small ridge and then runs due west across a level plain. After passing the *naveta* of Els Tudons and mounting a slight rise, the towers of Ciudadela come into sight, just peering above the creamy-white walls of the houses and apartment blocks which are now beginning to extend along the Mahon road.

Ciudadela

Ciudadela has been the centre of Christianity on Minorca since it was first introduced. When the wealth and importance of Roman Mahon vanished, the other centre at the western edge of the island managed to maintain itself as an urban community under successive dominations—probably Byzantine, certainly Muslim, and then Aragonese. Although there was no Christian bishop in Minorca between the Vandals of the fifth century and the end of the eighteenth century, the principal place of worship, whether Muslim or Christian, was always situated in Ciudadela. It was therefore natural that the principal civic authorities and the leading families of the island should establish themselves here. When Sir Richard Kane made Mahon capital of the island in 1722 instead of Ciudadela, the church and the aristocracy remained sturdily where they had always lived; and the situation is still the same today as a stroll through the inner part of the city will quickly reveal.

The inner area is divided from the outer by a wide avenue, running from the Plaza de Colon in the west and called at various points Negrete, Conquistador and José Antonio, as far as the Calle General Sanjurjo in the north of the town. Distances, however, are small as the total population today is only about 15,000. The streets on the outer side of the ring road are beginning to expand steadily—new warehouses, new apartments, new houses—but much of the inner city has changed little for generations, even centuries, with its cathedral, the great mansions of Minorca's nobility and the Borne, called Plaza del Generalissimo on the maps, which forms one of Spain's more impressive city centres. The wide avenue itself follows roughly what was originally the line of the city walls; these withstood the Turkish assault for nine days in 1558 and were largely razed to the ground as a result. Subsequently they were rebuilt at a leisurely pace from 1562 until the end of the seventeenth century, and were finally dismantled, this time for good, from 1868 onwards so that the town could expand. A fragment of the old defences can be seen supporting the Borne from the harbour side.

Perhaps the most important street in the old city starts from the Plaza Alfonso III, which faces the road to Mahon and the old windmill close by it. It then winds its way by the side of 'Ses Voltes' which are arcades with houses above. Here one can stroll out of the sun or rain, hold a market, or merely sit in a rocking chair and exchange gossip with a neighbour.

After passing the little Plaza España, the next stretch of this road, now named after the historian Quadrado, moves on to the cathedral, whose pale golden stone contrasts so felicitously with the whitewashed walls of the tall houses on the far side of the road. (It has changed its name again and is now called Pio XII.) The last stretch leads into the Borne, in the centre of which stands a graceful, slender obelisk. This monument was raised to commemorate the valiant defence of the city in 1558. On each side is a fountain whose jets of water rise and fall in the sultry summer air and give much pleasure to all who see them. Trees stand close to the obelisk and the fountains and give additional relief from the season's heat.

The tree-lined Paseo de San Nicolas is a much larger road; from the Borne it runs straight for nearly a kilometre until it reaches the sea and then swings to the south close to an ancient octagonal defence tower, standing a few feet above the sea on an uneven limestone platform. Opposite is an enormous modern hotel. Looking back to the city, one can see how flat the area is, and how haphazard the building.

Running parallel to the Paseo San Nicolas and immediately to its north are the waters of the port which flow inland as far as the Borne. The port itself faces west and is protected to some extent from the weather by a shoulder of land thrusting out to sea immediately to the north. There is moreover a wall on the north side of the quay to give protection from the north wind on *tramontana*. It was probably here that James the Conqueror's three ships were anchored when the Minorcan Arabs were presented with an ultimatum to become the king's vassals in 1235. Only small coastal vessels can berth in its shallow waters, including the passenger boats which travel to and from Alcudia in Majorca.

On the south side of the quay, where a road slopes up to the Borne near the Ayuntamiento, is a row of houses and cottages, one or two of which are cafés or restaurants. Some whitewashed, others in need of it, they face across the waters to similar houses which stare back at them from the far side of the harbour. At the edge of the quay a number of fishing and other small craft are moored. The weathered stones of Ciudadela are redolent of ancient families and their quarterings but the inhabitants wear this mantle of distinction lightly. Here, sitting at a café table by the harbour, there is a relaxed atmosphere and a feeling that there is no need to bother too much about outward appearances in a place where inner dignity is so deeply ingrained.

Of course the people of the city reflect something of its character in their behaviour. They are calm, unhurried and amicable, perhaps even more so than in Mahon where there is somewhat more bustle. Gaston Vuillier wrote, nearly 80 years ago, 'At Ciudadela the people are colder and more reserved, and their manners are solemn and sedate. The innkeeper hands you your soup with all the airs of a *grand seigneur*, and the chemist seems to pontificate as he hands you a seidlitz-powder. Your money is taken with the appearance of conferring a benefit on you. A French traveller observes', he adds, 'that this frigid manner is another trace of former British influence, but as a fact Mahon was the town most frequented by the English.' The inhabitants today are not cold, but have a reserve which is not unfriendly and which commands respect.

The quiet calmness of Ciudadela comes above all from the restrained splendour of its buildings, both ecclesiastical and domestic, and from the narrow streets which will only permit one-way traffic to move at a gentle pace. It does not naturally follow that every city has a cathedral worthy of it, but Ciudadela is fortunate. When the Muslims gained control of the island during the tenth century, they made Ciudadela their capital and built here their principal mosque. As in Palma and Ibiza, so in Ciudadela; as soon as the Catalan armies had triumphed, the principal Muslim mosque was declared Christian and services were at once celebrated there. It would naturally take sometime before the new Christian structure completely replaced the former mosque. By 1302, however, the new building was considerably advanced and was finished in 1362.

St. Mary of Ciudadela is, like the other two great cathedrals of the Balearic Islands in Palma and Ibiza, built in the Catalan—Gothic manner. The exterior has several features not dissimilar to Palma cathedral. There is a wall, an outer shell, which rises without windows from street level to well above the height of the west and south entrances. This may have been part of the fourteenth-century building or added after the destruction of the Turkish raid of 1558 in the hope that it might give some extra protection should a further attack occur; the little balustrade, with which this severe, uncompromising feature is capped, is Neo-classical. The actual restorations after 1558 were in Catalan—Gothic style, carried out over the following 150 years and consecrated in 1719. Behind and above the wall stand the thick square buttresses which are typical of the Catalan—Gothic style and in between them the light slender windows which rise to the cathedral roof.

There are two unusual features on the exterior of the cathedral. One is the tower on the north side, the bottom part of which formed part of the Muslim minaret attached to the original mosque; the ramp inside the tower is said to be typically Arabic. The other unusual feature, the west entrance, was built in an elegant Neo-classical style in 1813 but clashes with the Gothic of the rest of the edifice. The same lovely stone has fortunately been used throughout.

Inside, the vast, beautifully illumined golden interior consists of a single nave, without aisles, but with four chapels on the north side, one of them larger than the rest, and three on the south side together with the entrance. Nearly all of the interior embellishments were destroyed by Republican extremists during the 1936–39 Civil War; this explains the absence of a choir, pictures and other decorative features.

St. Mary's was raised to the status of a cathedral in 1795, many centuries after Makarius, the shadowy, last-recorded Bishop of Minorca, went in 484 to Carthage, then capital of the Vandal Kingdom, and was not heard of again. The Bishop's Palace stands in the Calle Obispo Torres, just to the north of the cathedral. The approach is through a gateway into a stone courtyard, surrounded by jasmin and other flowering shrubs and trees, massed beside the steps which lead up to the palace's entrance.

Not all of Ciudadela's churches are today used as places of worship. One in Obispo Vila has been converted into the offices and studios of Minorca's broadcasting station. Others which suffered damage during the Civil War have not yet been restored. One of the most remarkable in this category is the church of Our Lady of the Rosary in the Calle Rosario which at its north end faces the south side of the cathedral. The building of the church was started at the end of the seventeenth century by the Dominicans but before it was completed it was transformed into a Protestant place of worship for British troops. It is not possible to enter the church today but its west façade is much to be admired, in spite of the vandalism it suffered from the extreme Left during the Civil War. The two pairs of Solomonic pillars, one on each side of the entrance, which support the pediment, as well as other features of decorative ingenuity, have led writers to describe the main doorway as Churrigueresque in style.

St. Francis' at the south-east corner of the Borne continues in use as a church. It has a Gothic nave and side-chapels dating from the fourteenth century, but the east end of the church, together with the altar, are in the Baroque manner. The same contrast is to be found with regard to the exterior. The buttresses supporting the nave are Catalan–Gothic in style but at the eastern end is a seventeenth-century dome, enclosed in a square cube of masonry, as was often the custom in Majorca at this period. The church is built in the lovely, golden-yellow stone which has been widely used in Ciudadela. Another gem is the tiny Baroque chapel of Santo Cristo in the Calle Obispo Vila with its Classical columns and capitals and its octagonal stone dome surmounted by a little stone lantern. Light comes from its west window above the tiny gallery. On the north side of the altar is a carving of three saints on a dark red wooden panel. The church was restored in 1967 on its third centenary.

The seat of local government is in the Ayuntamiento or Town Hall, a brown, heavy civic structure on three floors with a squat tower complete with clock. The original building was destroyed in 1558 by the Turks and the restoration has not been too successful. Here are the mayor's offices and a small museum laid out not very methodically but with some interesting exhibits from the *Talayot* period onwards. These include Minorca's weights and measures stamped with the insignia of George III and some items associated with Admiral David Farragut. Here also, but in the mayor's office, is the Red Book, the *Llibre Vermell,* which contains the privileges granted by King Alfonso to the island, and which it has so jealously cherished ever since, together with Alfonso's battle standard. There is a fine view of the city from the roof, especially up the waters of the harbour to the Pla de Sant Joan (St. John's Field) and to the massive walls and buttresses of the cathedral whose pale-golden stone rises above the white walls of the surrounding houses.

The palaces and mansions of the Minorcan nobility are to be found in most parts of the inner city. One of the more picturesque is in the Borne facing the Ayuntamiento; this is the golden-brown Palace of el Conde (count) de Torre-Saura who is also Marqués de Moyá de la Torre. This palace, as well as the other two looking onto the Borne, was built at the beginning of the nineteenth century when an attempt was made to create a central square worthy of a capital city. At either end of a long two-storied building in the Neoclassical manner is a lofty open loggia, each with three arches. Separating them is the entrance, a tall, wooden door in a round, stone arch, surmounted by a coat of arms and a coronet, leading into a fine courtyard. In addition to possessing one of the largest reception rooms in the city, the palace is said to have a fine collection of watercolours and engravings from the period of the British occupation.

The palace of the Saura family in the Calle del Santissimo was built in the last third of the seventeenth century. Its exterior is finely proportioned and there are beatuifully wrought Neo-classical decorative features round the full-length windows on the first floor, the *piso principal,* each protected by a balcony. The broad stairway inside bears the date of 1718. The main reception rooms are spacious, lit by fine chandeliers from La Granja, near Madrid.

Also in the Calle del Santissimo is the palace of the Martorell family. Its distinguished but unadorned façade counter-balances the sonority and length of the owner's titles—the Marqués de Albranca, holding also the Dukedoms of Escalona and of Almenara-Alta, the Marquisates of La Lapilla, Villena, Paredes, Monesterio and Villel, the Counties of Alba de Liste and Ureña, and four times a Grandee of Spain.

The palace of the Barons de Lluriach, the most ancient of all the titles which originate in Minorca, stands in the Calle de Santa Clara, almost opposite the ancient convent of the Clares which Alfonso III founded in 1287. Except for some restrained decoration round the windows and the fine ironwork on the balconies, the exterior is absolutely plain, without even a coat of arms. This decorative restraint is to be found in most parts of Spain.

The fine mansion which stands opposite the west entrance to the cathedral belongs to the Olives family. Among its treasures is some fine Minorcan-made Georgian furniture, especially a remarkable set of dining chairs in the Chippendale style. There is also some excellent French eighteenth-century furniture which was added during the French domination of the island. Of particular interest is an enchanting monochrome frieze round the top of the walls in the three spacious state rooms; in one room it is devoted to birds, in another to beasts (with a flea standing next to an elephant), and in the third to fishes. This was the work of an unnamed French artist of the eighteenth century. The palace itself was built during the first third of the seventeenth century. A curious harmonium made by Longmans of Cheapside, London is there to be admired, as well as several good family portraits which indicate how much the families of the local nobility have intermarried. The wife of the ex-King Umberto of Italy passed a night here at the end of the 1939-45 war en route for Estoril, Portugal.

Also of interest is the mansion of the Squella family whose head is the Marqués de Menas Albas: it was here that Admiral Farragut spent the night during his visit to Ciudadela in December 1867. Particularly noteworthy is the wrought-iron staircase rail. Among other ancient families with mansions or palaces among the narrow streets which enfold the cathedral are those of Salort, Sintas, Olives and Vivo. There is also the fine house built at British expense for Don Juan-Miguel Saura, who had accompanied Stanhope in his attack on Minorca in 1708, to compensate him for the loss of his own house through the malice of the Bourbon opposition. It stands in Calle Obispo Vila and is now a bank.

The founders of several of these distinguished families may possibly have come to Minorca in 1287 with Alfonso III; one or two may even have been of knightly rank at that time. But it is even more certain that the great majority of these families were elevated to the nobility in the seventeenth and not the thirteenth century, a period when the status and trappings of nobility had a powerful appeal and much could be achieved by those who had honours to give. As a result of the Turkish destruction of the city of 1558, it was thought necessary to build new monasteries in Ciudadela in the seventeenth century. Father Miguel Subirats, a prior of the Augustine order, obtained permission from the royal court to offer deeds of nobility to those of good family in return for contributions made towards the building of the monastery of St. Augustine (San Angustin). The Order of the Clares was able to restore their convent which had also been destroyed in 1558 by the same means.

Today Ciudadela is perhaps known as much for its three-day celebrations of the Feast of St. John in June as for its ancient churches and palaces. The ceremony starts on the Sunday before the 24th June with a procession to the nearby Sanctuary of St. John, where a service is held. The procession is preceded by a man dressed in skins and bearing a live lamb on his shoulder, representing St. John the Baptist. After him ride the organizing committee, known as the *caixers*, of which the *caixer senyor*, who by tradition must be a nobleman, is the president; his official costume consists of full evening dress with white tie, though instead of trousers he wears white breeches and knee-high riding boots, and his head is crowned with a black two-pointed hat such as diplomats wear when in uniform. One of the most important aspects of the *Caixer Senyor*'s work is to entertain his colleagues generously, especially at the party given after the parade of horses on St. John's Day. He is traditionally chosen from one of eight families only. The rest of the committee consists of a representative of the church; two agricultural and one industrial worker, the last of whom carries the banner of St. John with its Maltese Cross; the *caixer Fadri*, representing unmarried youth; and the *Fabioler* who, mounted on a stallion, plays the fife and kettledrum to indicate changes in direction of the procession.

During these festivities various games and contests on horse-back are played in the Pla de Sant Joan, close to where the waters of the port end. The crowning point of all, however, is the formal prancing on horseback of the *Caixers* and other horsemen round the Borne and through the city. Similar festivals take place elsewhere on the island, to which they are unique, but that of Ciudadela is by far the best known and a source of great pride to the community.

To the south of Ciudadela lies a flat, rocky countryside made up of small green fields, stone walls and many new villas close to the sea, where there are one or two good beaches. At Cap d'Artrutx at the southern end of the coastline, is a lighthouse. On the rocky foreshore apartments, houses and one or two hotels are being energetically constructed. The same is true of the coast around Cap de Banyos, immediately to the west of Ciudadela, but not from Cap de Bajoli to Cala Morell because here there are no beaches to encourage developers.

Cala Morell, with its cliffs, sandy beach, prehistoric caves and new houses, can be reached by a good road from Ciudadela in about fifteen minutes. Roads have been laid out on the bare cliff tops but few villas have as yet been built here. Much further back among the pinewoods are a number of elaborate white villas. Cala Morell is wonderfully sited for the hot, still, breathless days of summer, but the *tramontana* can blow as late as April to the accompaniment of pounding seas and clouds of stinging misty spray. Minorca is an exciting island.

Bibliography

A. SPANISH HISTORY AND GENERAL

Boardman, John, *The Greeks Overseas*, London 1964
Bouchier, E. S., *Spain under the Roman Empire*, Oxford 1914
Braudel, Fernand, *The Mediterranean and the Mediterranean World in the Age of Philip II*, 2 vols., London 1972–3
Carpenter, Rhys, *The Greeks in Spain*, London 1925
Chaytor, H. J., *History of Aragon and Catalonia*, London 1933
Elliott, J. H., *Imperial Spain, 1469–1716*, London 1963
Rossello Bordoy, Guillem, *L'Islam a les Illes Balears*, Palma de Mallorca 1968
Runciman, Sir Steven, *The Sicilian Vespers*, Cambridge 1958
Thomas, Hugh, *The Spanish Civil War*, London 1961

B. ROMAN WRITERS

Livy, *History of Rome*
Siculus, Diodorus, *Bibliotheca Historica*
Strabo, *Geography*
Tacitus, *Annals*

C. IBIZA AND MINORCA

Armstrong, John, *History of the Island of Minorca*, London 1752
Boyd, Mary Stuart, *Fortunate Isles*, London 1911
Camps, Fernando Marti, *History of Menorca*, Menorca 1971
Chamberlin, F., *The Balearics and their Peoples*, London 1927
Colas, Jean, *The Balearics: Islands of Enchantment*, London 1967
Dameto and Mut, *The Ancient and Modern History of the Balearic Islands*, trans. by Colin Campbell, London 1716

Flitch, J. E. Crawford, *Mediterranean Moods,* London 1911
Grasset de St. Sauveur, André, *Voyages dans les Isles Baleares,* Paris 1807
Lamiere, Irénée, *Les Occupations Militaires de l'Isle de Minorque,* Paris 1908
Macabich Llobet, Canon Isidoro, *Historia de Ibiza,* Palma de Mallorca, 1930 etc.
McGuffee, T. H., 'The Defence of Minorca', vol. 10, *History Today,* London 1951
Markham, Sir Clements R., *Majorca and Minorca,* London 1908
Paul, Elliott, *The Life and Death of a Spanish Town,* London 1937
Pons, Guillermo, *Historia de Menorca,* Minorca, 1971
Villangomez, Maria, *Llibre d'Eivissa,* Barcelona 1957
Vuillier, Gaston, *The Forgotten Isles,* trans. by F. Breton, London 1896
Whelpton, Eric, *The Balearics,* London 1952

D. BIOGRAPHIES, CHRONICLES, etc.

Bradford, Ernle, *The Sultan's Admiral,* London 1969
Dictionary of National Biography
Hervey, Augustus, *Journal,* ed. by David Erskine, London 1953
James I, King of Aragon, *The Chronicle,* trans. by J. Forster, London 1883
Mahan, Captain A. T., *Admiral Farragut,* London 1893
Mahan, Captain A. T., *The Life of Nelson,* London 1897
Murray, Geoffrey, *The Life of Admiral Collingwood,* London 1936
Nouvelle Biographie Generale
Parry, Anne, *The Admirals Fremantle,* London 1971
Pope, Dudley, *At 12 Mr Byng was Shot,* London 1962
Williams, Basil, *Stanhope: A Study in Eighteenth Century War and Diplomacy,* Oxford 1922

E. ARCHITECTURE, ARCHAEOLOGY AND THE ARTS

Almegro Gorbea, Maria José, *Guia del Puig des Molins, Ibiza,* Madrid 1969
Foss, Arthur, *Majorca,* London 1972
Harden, Donald, *The Phoenicians,* London 1962

Lavedan, Pierre, *Palma de Majorque,* Paris 1936
Mascaro Pasarius, J., *Prehistoria de las Balears,* Palma de Mallorca, 1968
Moscati, Sabatino, *The World of the Phoenicians,* London 1968
Murray, Margaret A., *Cambridge Excavations in Minorca,* Cambridge 1938
Pericot Garcia, L., *The Balearic Islands,* London 1972
Post, Chandler R., *History of Spanish Painting,* Cambridge, Mass. 1930 etc.

F. MISCELLANEOUS

Fortescue, the Hon. J. W., *A History of the British Army,* London 1899
Marshall, F. H., 'A Greek Community in Minorca', *The Slavonic and Eastern Review,* Vol. 11, 1932
Three contemporary pamphlets:
A Faithful and Authentic Report of the Siege and Surrender of St. Philip's Fort in the Island of Minorca, printed for C. Crowder & H. Woodgate, London, 1757
An Account of the Facts which appeared on the late Enquiry into the Loss of Minorca, from Authentic Papers by the Monitor, printed for J. Scott, London, 1757
A Full Account of the Siege of Minorca by the French in 1756 with all the Circumstances Relating Thereto, printed for A. & C. Corbett in Fleet Street, London
Papers in the Public Record Office, London W.C.2.
Acknowledgements are made to the excellent series of monographs on the art, history, literature and life of the Balearic Islands under the general direction of Senor Don Luis Ripoll Arbos, published in the series *Panorama Balear,* Palma de Mallorca.

Index

F after a place name indicates Formentera, I Ibiza, M Minorca and Ma Majorca

Index

Index

Index